CRACKING *Writing*

Teacher's Guide

Kate Ruttle

RISING★STARS

YEAR 3

Hachette UK's policy is to use papers that are natural, renewable and recyclable products and made from wood grown in sustainable forests. The logging and manufacturing processes are expected to conform to the environmental regulations of the country of origin.

Orders: please contact Bookpoint Ltd, 130 Park Drive, Milton Park, Abingdon, Oxon OX14 4SE. Telephone: (44) 01235 400555. Email primary@bookpoint.co.uk.

Lines are open from 9 a.m. to 5 p.m., Monday to Saturday, with a 24-hour message answering service. Visit our website at www.risingstars-uk.com for details of the full range of Rising Stars publications.
Online support and queries:
Email: onlinesupport@risingstars-uk.com

ISBN: 978-1-51040-199-0

Text, design and layout © 2017 Rising Stars UK Ltd
First published in 2017 by Rising Stars UK Ltd
Rising Stars UK Ltd, part of Hodder Education Group
An Hachette UK Company
Carmelite House, 50 Victoria Embankment, London EC4Y 0DZ
www.risingstars-uk.com
Impression number   10 9 8 7 6 5 4 3 2 1
Year   2020 2019 2018 2017

Author: Kate Ruttle
Publishers: Laura White and Nick Hunter
Illustrator: Clair Rossiter, Bright Group International
Text design, logo and cover design: Julie Martin
Typesetting: Aptara Inc.
Copy Editor: Lesley Densham
Proofreader: Debbie Allen
Project editor: Rachel Nickolds
Printed by: Ashford Colour Press Ltd.

A catalogue record for this title is available from the British Library.

Acknowledgements

Every effort has been made to trace all copyright holders, but if any have been inadvertently overlooked, the Publishers will be pleased to make the necessary arrangements at the first opportunity.

Although every effort has been made to ensure that website addresses are correct at time of going to press, Rising Stars cannot be held responsible for the content of any website mentioned in this book. It is sometimes possible to find a relocated web page by typing in the address of the home page for a website in the URL window of your browser.

The Publishers would like to thank the following for permission to reproduce copyright material.

Text acknowledgements

p6 *Scout and the Sausage Thief* by Gill Leiws; p17 *The Disappearing Moon* by Simon Bartram; p29 *Frankie vs the Pirate Pillagers* by Frank Lampard; p40 *Storm* by Kevin Crossley-Holland; p84 *The Stick Book: Loads of Things You Can Make or Do With a Stick* by Jo Schofield and Fiona Danks; p95 *The Teacher's Day in Bed* by David Orme © David Orme, reproduced by kind permission.

Photo acknowledgements

t = top; **b** – bottom; **l** = left; **r** = right; **c** = centre

p52 Sergey Uryadnikov/Shutterstock; p53t Chatchai Somwat/Shutterstock; p53b Maynard Case/Shutterstock; p73 Monika Surzin/Shutterstock; p74t Mark Caunt/Shutterstock; p74b Will Howe/Shutterstock; p84 Inc/Shutterstock; p85 Oleg Mikhaylov /Shutterstock.

Contents

Introduction

What is *Cracking Writing*?

Cracking Writing is a step-by-step resource to improve children's composition and writing skills. The advice and guidance in this *Teacher's Guide* will help you to teach children the skills and strategies they need to write effectively for a wide range of purposes. The approach combines creativity and intention with a thorough understanding of grammar in context, and will enable you to successfully deliver the expectations of the 2014 National Curriculum for English.

Cracking Writing can be used to support most approaches to writing which recognise the benefit and importance of:

- reading and responding to model texts
- talk for writing and planning writing
- planning, drafting, editing and improving writing.

What's in it?

Cracking Writing offers nine writing units for each Year: four fiction units, four non-fiction units and one poetry unit. The units have been chosen to support the expectations of the National Curriculum for Key Stage 2 English. The units, and in particular the non-fiction units, can also be used as resources to enrich and complement your wider teaching. Each unit includes:

- a model text
- a reading comprehension activity in order to ensure close reading and comprehension of the model text
- active learning activities and guidance for six stages of teaching writing
- a framework for writing
- a detailed moderating writing sheet which shows progression from 'below the expected standard' to 'working at greater depth' for the standard expected by the end of the academic year.

> Visit My Rising Stars online (**www.risingstars-uk. com**) to access your extra resources. These include:
>
> - model texts highlighted with key grammatical constructions
> - editable success criteria.

The text types and purposes of the units in *Cracking Writing* mirror those in Rising Stars' *Cracking Comprehension*. Each of the resources stands alone and is in no way dependent on the other, but schools that have both resources can add value to them by:

- seeing how well the children are able to apply strategies taught in *Cracking Comprehension* when faced with the new *Cracking Writing* text and additional comprehension questions
- using the *Cracking Comprehension* texts as additional model texts through which to explore the issues raised in *Cracking Writing* units.

How do I use it?

You can use the *Cracking Writing* units in any order. The pathway through each unit is flexible, according to the specific needs of you and your children. Whether you choose to follow through with one stage every day for six or seven days, or weekly for half a term or for a focused half day per half-term is your choice. The children will gain more from the sessions if they are closer together, but the decision rests with you – you know your class.

Each unit is divided into the same six stages. Depending on your own emphasis and the class's needs, you can allocate a lesson to each of the stages. You may wish to leave out some of the activities which don't address your priorities, but do check that the learning isn't needed for later in the unit.

However you choose to use the material, we recommend that you follow this process:

Stage 1: Introduce, read and respond to the model text

Each unit is based on a model text. These are generally extracts from good quality, age-appropriate children's fiction, non-fiction and poetry. Introductory activities start the children thinking about the subject matter of the text. Ideas generated are often used in a later stage.

Discussing children's responses to the model text and the comprehension questions will ensure the children are very familiar with the text for subsequent stages.

Stage 2: Analyse the text content (fiction)/analyse the text structure and organisation (non-fiction)

During this stage, children are asked to consider the setting, character and plot in the fiction model texts, and to explore the organisation, the order of ideas and the use of headings and other text features for the non-fiction texts. Children will work with response partners and groups for active learning activities aimed at co-constructing insights into the author's choices and their impact on the reader.

Stage 3: Analyse the text structure and language (fiction)/analyse the text purpose and language (non-fiction)

Activities in this stage are primarily focused on language and the grammatical content and technical vocabulary for Year 3 in the National Curriculum, together with consolidation of grammatical content and vocabulary from previous years. The intention is to demonstrate how the grammar is used in texts and to consider the impact on the reader. Key grammatical constructions are highlighted on the model text (online at My Rising Stars). Paragraphs and vocabulary are also considered in most units.

There are lots of opportunities for children to work in pairs or groups in order to encourage discussion and debate and to give all children the opportunity to share their ideas. You can decide whether you wish to work with a group of less confident children, or whether you wish to pair them with more confident peers.

Stage 4: Plan to write (including talk for writing)

The aim of this stage is to discuss ideas and create opportunities for drama, drawing, internet research, and so on so that children come to the writing session with a clear understanding of the content, style and vocabulary of what they want to write, whether the recommendation is a continuation of the model text or a piece of writing inspired by it.

- A framework for writing offers the children one way of recording key ideas they will find useful. A range of photocopiable frameworks is provided and some may be adaptable for use in other units.
- Each unit includes opportunities to 'talk like a writer'.
- Editable success criteria are available online at My Rising Stars. Agree and share the success criteria with the children.

Stage 5: Write (including talk for writing)

By the end of this stage, children will have completed their first draft, using their completed frameworks, results of 'talk like a writer' sessions and success criteria discussed at the previous stage. The activities give guidance on supporting the writing process and give children opportunities to read, and make first corrections to their work.

- 🖥 This symbol is used to suggest where writing activities are particularly suited to being written on PCs/laptops/tablets.

Stage 6: Improve, edit and share the writing

For many children, it is the activities undertaken during this stage that have the greatest impact on their development as writers. They have recorded their ideas, so can now proofread, correct and improve their texts.

Photocopiable moderating writing sheets are provided on which you can highlight aspects of writing where children are working at the expected level and those which are below the expected level or working at greater depth. Each moderating writing sheet is slightly different to reflect the success criteria, and all reflect end-of-year expectations as the units can be completed in any order. During the first half of the year, most children will appear to be below expected levels.

Scout and the Sausage Thief

Gill Lewis

> *Scout goes to Puppy Academy where she is learning to be a police dog. On the day of a big test about helping people in the community, Scout didn't want to be late.*

Scout set off again. She was weaving her way in and out of parents with pushchairs and children on their way to school when she suddenly stumbled on something on the ground.

It was a threadbare teddy with a missing eye and a sticking plaster on its paw. It lay in a puddle with a big muddy footprint on its tummy. It looked sad and lonely. Scout sniffed it. Beneath the mud and water, it smelled of strawberry shampoo and cheese and pickle sandwiches.

Scout knew that someone loved this teddy. She looked around to see if she could see anyone looking for it, but everyone was hurrying to get out of the rain.

A human child must have dropped this on the way to school, she thought. Maybe she should take it to the school, but that would make her late for her test. Maybe she should leave it here. Whoever lost it might find it on the way home.

Scout sat the teddy on a bench and walked on, but deep inside she just knew that someone wanted this teddy back. She couldn't leave it. Scout turned around, picked up the teddy and trotted to the school. She followed the long line of children to the school gates. A small girl smelling of strawberry shampoo was sobbing in her mother's arms.

Scout trotted up and pushed the teddy into the girl's hands.

"Eddie," cried the girl, "you're alive!" She hugged her teddy tight against her.

"Clever pup," said the girl's mother, patting Scout on the head. "However did you find him?"

Scout wanted to tell her where she'd found the teddy, but she knew humans didn't understand woofs and barks, so she just wagged her tail instead.

The girl reached into her bag and offered Scout a cheese and pickle sandwich, but at that moment the school bell rang and Scout knew it was time for her to go to school too.

Unit 1: Scout and the Sausage Thief

Name: Class: Date:

1. Who is Scout? Tick **one**.

   a girl   ☐   a puppy   ☐

   a police officer   ☐   a teddy   ☐

2. How did Scout know someone loved the teddy?

   _____

3. Why didn't Scout leave the teddy on the bench?

   _____

4. How did Scout know when she had found the teddy's owner?

   _____

   _____

5. Why do you think the girl offered Scout a sandwich?

   _____

6. Number these events 1–4 to show the order in which they happened.

   The first one has been done for you.

   Scout saw the teddy in a puddle.   ☐ 1

   The school bell rang.   ☐

   Scout put the teddy on a bench.   ☐

   Scout took the teddy to the school.   ☐

Unit 1 Writing a story about a character

In this unit children will:

- read a model text with a strong central character
- explore how the author creates character with explicit (told) and implicit (inferred) information
- identify the main sections of the text, considering how paragraphs are used to organise and link ideas
- discover how the author links ideas, and adds new information using adverbs and conjunctions to tell us about changes in time and place
- plan, draft, edit and improve a new story with the same central character.

Stage 1: Responding to the text

Activities:

- Establish prior knowledge.
  - Have any of the children read any of the *Puppy Academy* books? If so, allow them to share their experiences.
  - *Think, pair, share:* What are the children's expectations of characters in a series called *Puppy Academy*?
- Introduce the text. Explain that the two sentences in italics at the top of the page are there because this text is an extract (a short part) of a longer book, and the introduction is meant to give you information that you need to know in order to understand events in the extract.
- Before reading the story, ensure the children understand the meaning of the more unusual words and phrases: *"weaving"*, *"threadbare"*, *"deep inside"*, *"community"* and *"police dog"*. Explain the meaning of these words in the context of the story. Help the children to remember the meanings of these words by putting them in contextualising sentences, e.g. *She was sad because deep inside she knew she wouldn't see her teddy again.*
- Read and talk about the text. Ask the children:
  - What do you think Scout was thinking about as she was on her way?
  - Why did she stop when she saw the teddy?
  - What might have happened if a different dog had seen the teddy? What if it was a sad dog? Or an angry dog?
- Ask the children to answer the reading comprehension questions to ensure close reading of the text and good understanding. Ensure they understand how to answer the types of questions asked. If necessary, model how to find and copy words from the text and how to add numbers in the sequencing question.
- Together, share answers to the questions and discuss the strategies children used to answer them. Talk about how to find the evidence in the story for question 4. Show the children that there is more than one reason that we know Scout has found the right child.

Resources needed:

Shared copy of the text (PDF/IWB/visualiser)

Each child needs:

- a copy of the text
- a copy of the comprehension questions.

Stage 2: Analysing the text content

Activities:

- Ask children to read the text aloud to a response partner to revisit the text, develop fluency, ensure appropriate pronunciation of all words and to practise reading with good intonation and expression.
- Ask children to underline any new words or phrases. Take feedback and explain what these mean in context.

Discussing character

- Model finding a piece of information and making an inference from it (e.g. *"Scout knew someone loved this teddy"* tells us that Scout knows about children and she cares about them and their teddies).
- Ask groups of children to use a large sheet of paper to list everything they know about Scout. Ask them to note down ideas about her:
  - appearance (e.g. *young/a puppy*)
  - skills (e.g. *good at tracking and sniffing; good at weaving and trotting; quite fit*)
  - ambition (e.g. *keen; wants to do well; wants to be a police dog*)
  - character (e.g. *kind; caring; wants to help; clever; knows about humans*).
    - Challenge children to tell you how they know the answers to these questions. Where did they find the information?
- Talk about the fact that we don't know what Scout looks like.
  - Show children images of the dogs. Ask them to vote for the one they think is the best match for Scout (not for their favourite dog!). Talk about what it is about the pictures that makes children think this is Scout.
  - Does it matter in this text that we don't know what Scout looks like? Point out that if it was important, the author would have told the reader. (*Agree that it can be helpful for visualising the characters in the story but it's not important for the actions. If children are worried about it, tell them that the author thinks of Scout as a German Shepherd.*)
- Ask children if they think it's OK to leave descriptions to the reader's imagination, or if they prefer a full description.

Resources needed:

Shared copy of the text (PDF/IWB/visualiser)

Shared images of dogs: Labrador, German Shepherd, collie, pug, dachshund, toy poodle

Each group needs:

- large paper
- an enlarged copy of the text

Each child needs:

- a copy of the text
- different coloured highlighters/pens/pencils.

Discussing plot

- Remind children of the most common 'shape' of a story:
  - Introduction – we're given background information
  - Problem – we're introduced to the reason for the events in the story
  - Action – the main characters do or think something
  - Outcome – what happens after the action
  - Ending – tidies up all the ideas.
- Clarify that the introduction to the whole story isn't given here, but the important parts are included in italics in paragraph 1.
- In their groups, ask children to discuss their ideas about which paragraphs match which part of the text. Then use the enlarged copy of the text to circle different parts of the story in different colours.
  - Clarify that there is no 'right' answer to the question and the answers are likely to vary a bit, but may include:
    - introduction – paragraph 1 in italics
    - problem – paragraphs 2–5
    - action – paragraphs 6 (beginning *"Scout sat"*), 7 and 8 (ending *"hugged her teddy tight against her"*)
    - outcome – paragraphs 9 (beginning *"Clever pup"*) and 10 (ending *"wagged her tail instead"*)
    - ending – final paragraph.
- Remind children that this is an episode in a longer book.
  - Ask them in their groups to talk about how they could make the action part of the text more exciting, and then to consider how that would affect the outcome and ending.

Stage 3: Analysing the text structure and language

Resources needed:

Shared copy of the text (PDF/IWB/visualiser)

Each pair needs:

• an enlarged copy of the text

Each child needs:

• the copy of the text they have previously highlighted and annotated

• different coloured pens/pencils.

Activities:

Looking at paragraphs

• Ask children how they would feel if all of this text was presented as a block. Would they want to read it?

• *Think, pair, share:* Why do writers use paragraphs? (E.g. *to organise and link ideas clearly for the reader; to introduce new sections of a story; to show when a new speaker is talking.*)

  ○ Introduce a list of common reasons for beginning new paragraphs:

  (a) new speaker in dialogue

  (b) new/change of event or action

  (c) new/change of place

  (d) new/change of time

  (e) new/change of character.

  ○ In pairs, ask children to write a number beside each paragraph of the enlarged copy of the story, indicating why the author began a new paragraph (e.g. *paragraph 1 (introduction): e; paragraph 2: b; paragraph 3: b paragraph 4: a; paragraph 5: a; paragraph 6: c; paragraph 7: b; paragraph 8: a; paragraph 9: a; paragraph 10: b; paragraph 11: b*).

• Clarify that paragraphs are useful for making a text look less scary to read, but they also help the reader to understand the sequence of events and ideas.

Looking at time and place

• Remind children that verbs are words that tell you what a character *did, was* or *had.*

  ○ Model looking for verbs in the opening paragraph (e.g. *"goes", "is learning", "didn't want"*).

  ○ Can children find some verbs in paragraphs 2–4? (E.g. *"was weaving", "stumbled", "was", "lay", "looked", "sniffed", "smelled", "knew", "loved", "looked", "see", "was hurrying".*)

• Can the children tell you what adverbs do in a sentence? (E.g. *They tell you more about the verb and explain when, where or how an action happened.*)

  ○ Model looking for adverbs of place in the text (e.g. *"Beneath; "(trotted) up"; "(walked) on"; "(looked) around"*) and help children to identify which verbs they tell you more about.

  ○ *Think, pair, share:* Ask children to look in the text for: an adverb of time (e.g. *suddenly, at that moment*). Can children tell you which verb the adverbs tell you more about?

  ○ Talk about the importance of adverbs in helping the reader to understand what's happening in a story. (*Although adverbs of manner add details, adverbs of time and place are important in helping the reader to keep track of when and where events happen.*)

• Can the children tell you what conjunctions do in a sentence? (E.g. *Express time, place and cause while joining sentences, phrases or clauses together.*)

  ○ Model finding a conjunction in the opening paragraph (*"where"*). Point out to children that there is a verb in the clause before the conjunction and a verb in the clause after it.

  ○ *Think, pair, share:* Ask children to look in the text for three more conjunctions (e.g. *but, and, so, where, when, for*). Each time, they should be able to find a verb in the clause before the conjunction and another verb in the clause after it.

  ○ Talk about the importance of conjunctions so the reader understands when, where and why things happen.

Looking at dialogue

- Ask children to identify where in the text we first meet speech, or dialogue. (*"Eddie," cried the girl, "you're alive!"*)
  - Can children identify how they knew that it is dialogue? (*Layout and use of inverted commas.*)
  - In pairs, ask children to use the enlarged text and underline the words that the girl actually said in one colour, and the words her mother said in another.
  - Ask children to explain how they knew who said what, e.g.
    - inverted commas are around the words that were said
    - the phrases *"cried the girl"* and *"said the girl's mother"* tell you who was speaking.
- Talk about why the reader needs the punctuation. *(So they know how to read the text.)*
  - Ask children to read the text aloud again to their response partner while they focus on how the punctuation helps them to understand how to read the text.

Stage 4: Planning to write: Writing a story about a character

Activities:

- Ask children to read the text aloud to a response partner while thinking how paragraphs and punctuation help the reader to read with fluency and expression.

Thinking about story ideas

- Tell children that they are going to write their own story about Scout.
- In groups, ask children to revisit the notes they made about Scout's character. Remind them that they noted down words and phrases, not whole sentences.
- Work together as a class to make a few notes – using words and phrases, not whole sentences – of other ideas for stories involving Scout. Remind children that they need to keep using what they already know of her character.
- Give each group a large sheet of paper and ask them to think about other different stories about Scout. Tell them that their story ideas should:
  - use the same character of Scout as in the model text (so she can't be a villain)
  - be somehow related to her work as a trainee police dog (e.g. *solving a crime; finding something; catching a robber*).
- Ask children to brainstorm ideas. One child from each group should scribe the group's ideas in words and phrases only – not in full sentences.
- Allow groups to look at the ideas other groups have suggested.
- Explain that story writing is not a competition and that all writers borrow ideas and words from other writers. If someone borrows your idea, it's because it was a good idea so you can be proud. They will change your idea in their own story anyway.

Planning in pairs

- Distribute the writing framework.
  - Remind children that this isn't their story and should not be written in sentences. The limited amount of space provided is all they should need.
- Together, model taking one of the ideas from the children's papers and talking through how the idea needs to be planned into sections to show the different stages in the story.
- Working in pairs, the children should add as much detail as is useful to their plan.

Resources needed:

Shared copy of the text (PDF/IWB/visualiser)

The success criteria

Groups of children need:

- the large paper on which they recorded details of Scout's character
- another large sheet of paper

Each child needs:

- the copy of the text they have previously highlighted and annotated
- marker pens or coloured pencils
- the writing framework from page 15 (some children may benefit from this being enlarged to A3).

- Give each child the opportunity to 'talk like a writer' to a different response partner, to say how they think the story will develop and to receive peer feedback.
- Ask the children to say what they think the new story about Scout should include.
- Clarify and amend the success criteria (online at My Rising Stars) if appropriate.

Stage 5: Writing

Activities:

- Remind children that they are writing a new story about Scout the police dog trainee.
- Model using your plan to write part of your story. Ensure you include adverbs of time and place, joining two clauses together with a coordinating conjunction and adding information using a subordinating conjunction, as well as some dialogue to show a character's reaction to Scout's behaviour.

Resources needed:

The success criteria

Each child needs:

- the copy of the text they have previously highlighted and annotated
- the completed writing framework.

- Give children a few minutes to 'talk like a writer' and tell another response partner the story as they plan to write it. If it helps, ask them to use a polite 'writer's voice'. Remind them to use their plan and not to invent another story as they go along.
- Remind children they can compose and rehearse sentences inside their head or in a low whisper before they begin to write them.
- Let response partners give some brief feedback before children swap roles.
- Tell children your expectations about how much space each part of the story will take up on the page, e.g.
  - introduction: 2–3 lines
  - problem: 4–5 lines
  - action: 4–5 lines
  - outcome: 3–4 lines
  - ending: 2–3 lines.

  (Amend these line numbers for your class and the amount of time they have to write.)
- Read aloud the success criteria (online at My Rising Stars).
- Let the children write. Break up the process, paragraph by paragraph. Remind children that they can use different sentence types, dialogue or they can start sentences with an adverb.
- Five minutes before the end of the stage, ask all children to stop writing and read their story aloud to themselves. If they find errors, missing words or words they can improve, they should use this opportunity to make changes.

Stage 6: Improving, editing, reviewing and sharing the writing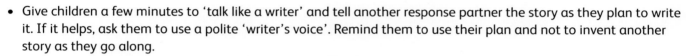

Activities:

- Revisit together the success criteria (online at My Rising Stars).
- Model the process below using your work as an example. The children can give you feedback on each step of the process. After you model a step, the children should have a go with their partner at editing their own work.

Resources needed:

Each child needs:

- the success criteria
- their writing/completed writing framework
- different coloured highlighters/pens/pencils.

- Ask children to reread their texts three times with their response partner:
  - First read through: Children read their partner's text out loud to them. The child who wrote the text listens to check that their writing makes sense, listens out for obvious errors and checks the text follows their plan. Children then swap roles.

o Second read through: Children read their partner's text and highlight the success criteria they have met. They suggest three places where their partner could improve their work (to achieve or further improve on the success criteria).

o Third read through: Children proofread their partner's text together with them. They check for errors in punctuation and spelling, and correct these as necessary. You should give input at this stage if needed.

Lessons from writing

Prior to the session, identify errors that were commonly made. Write sample sentences that need to be corrected and ask the children to help you to fix them. These could include:

- a string of simple sentences with no conjunctions, e.g. *Scout saw something moving. She ran and hid behind a chair. She thought she saw something under the table. She gave a loud bark. Someone ran out of the room.* Explore different ways of joining these sentences with coordinating conjunctions (e.g. *and, or* and *but*) or making one clause subordinate by putting a subordinating conjunction with it (e.g. *when, until*). Again, discuss the impact.

- no new line and no punctuation for dialogue, e.g. *What are you doing there? said the big guard dog. Looking for my friend, said Scout. Well she's not here so go away said the big dog.* Ask children to help you to organise and present the dialogue appropriately. Can they suggest better verbs than *said*?

Improving the writing

- **After the stories have been marked:** give the children time to read through your comments, to look at the success criteria and to implement any changes suggested. This should not involve the children rewriting the entire story – just those parts that you would like them to revisit to practise/improve their writing.

Share

Sometimes, children write stories to practise writing stories. Other times, there is a planned reason or an audience. If you want children to share their writing:

- they can rewrite it to presentation standards; however, this should be regarded simply as a handwriting activity, not as another opportunity to improve the text – the rewritten text should be used for a specific audience or display

- they could work in a group to share ideas and create a short playscript to present with puppets

- they could contribute their story to your own *Puppy Academy* book with Scout stories

- if there are some good ideas, you could send them to Oxford University Press for Gill Lewis to look at.

Unit 1: Writing a story about a character

Name: Class: Date:

In the table below, write notes for each paragraph of your story about Scout.

Introduction: Introduce the characters.	
Problem: What is the story going to be about?	
Action: What is the main event going to be?	
Outcome: What happens next?	
Ending: How does the story finish?	

Unit 1: Moderating writing: Writing a story about a character

Name: Date:

	Contents	Text structure and organisation	Sentence structure	Vocabulary and descriptions	Punctuation	Spelling and handwriting
Working at greater depth within the expected standard	Characters and settings are consistent and convincing.	Paragraphs introduce a change of speaker, time, place or action.	The story is consistently in the past tense, except in dialogue.	More sophisticated vocabulary is used to create atmosphere.	Inverted commas and other punctuation are used in dialogue.	Spelling changes needed to add vowel suffixes are often accurate.
	At least one additional detail is included to help the reader to engage with the text.	The story has a satisfying shape leading to an exciting action, outcome and ending.	Appropriate choice of pronouns is used to avoid repetition.	Noun phrases may be extended with prepositional phrases.	Apostrophes are only used in appropriate contexts.	In handwriting, most letters are appropriately joined or word-processing speed is developing and does not impede thought processes.
Working at the expected standard	A new detective story is written about Scout.	Paragraphs are used to distinguish different sections in the story.	Some sentences begin with an adverb to show a change of time or place.	Expanded noun phrases are used to describe setting and character.	Inverted commas are used in dialogue.	A range of prefixes and suffixes is used.
			The text includes at least two different types of sentence.		Apostrophes are used to show possession (singular).	Taught spellings from the Year 3/4 word list are correct.
	Some attempt is made to develop character and setting.	The story leads towards a single interesting event.	A range of coordinating and subordinating conjunctions link clauses.	Descriptive verbs make the action fast paced.	End of sentence punctuation (.?!) is generally accurate.	Some letters are joined using diagonal or horizontal strokes.
					Commas are used to separate items in lists.	Letters and spaces are in proportion to each other.
Working towards the expected standard	The story follows the plan.	Ideas are grouped and sequenced appropriately.	At least three different conjunctions are used correctly.	Some expanded noun phrases are used.	End of sentence punctuation (.?!) is often accurate.	Spelling errors are phonetically decodable.
	The story is about Scout the dog.		Most of the story is in the past tense.		Apostrophes are used for contractions (missing letters).	Spaces between letters and words allow for good legibility.

The Disappearing Moon

Simon Bartram

> *Bob, the Man on the Moon, was tidying up the space tourists' rubbish in a hurry because he wanted to get back to Earth quickly. Bob didn't believe in aliens, so no aliens could have been watching him (could they?). He had always wanted to see The Stupendous Alacazamo's spectacular live magic show and he had tickets for the eight o'clock performance. He was so excited he could hardly fly his rocket straight.*

Having landed back at the Lunar Hill launch-pad, Bob quickly popped into his changing cubicle. In a super-fast flash, he shoved on his Earth clothes and cycled home as quickly as his legs would take him. It wasn't until later that he realised he hadn't put on his vest.

At home, after a speedy wash and brush up, he wolfed down some fish-paste sandwiches and selected his favourite mesmerising swirl badge to wear. "Perfect!" he beamed.

Bob then dug out the precious tickets that were hidden in an old biscuit tin between the sheets in the airing cupboard. He'd saved for months to buy them and had even sold his third-best tank top to raise some extra money.

"Nights out don't come cheap, Barry," he said. "Especially if you fancy getting a souvenir T-shirt or a choc-ice."

It was almost time to set off. All Bob had to do was find his autograph book and set his trusty old video to record the football.

The streets outside were buzzing. It seemed as if the whole town was off to see the show. The Moon shone brightly overhead as Bob and Barry set off down the road. As the Glitterball Theatre came into view, butterflies began to swirl around Bob's tummy. His legs wobbled as he walked through the theatre's grand, pillared entrance and into the beautiful auditorium.

He and Barry were the first to take their seats, but soon the theatre filled up around them. Then, at eight o'clock, the lights dimmed. A huge cheer filled the auditorium before it was replaced by an electric hush. In the darkness, a thousand eyes could just make out the heavy, velvet curtains swishing open. Bob's heart was racing. Suddenly, a tremendous bang and a flash of lightning made the whole audience jump. A hundred spotlights cut through the darkness and revealed a cloud of smoke swirling around the stage. The audience "OOOHED!" and "AAAHED!" as the silhouette of a caped figure began to emerge through the haze.

For Bob it was a dream come true. In front of his very eyes, there he was at last … THE STUPENDOUS ALACAZAMO!!!

Unit 2: The Disappearing Moon

1. What was Bob so excited about?

    _____

2. *"Bob then dug out the precious tickets ..."*

    Why were the tickets so precious to Bob? Tick **one**.

    He hid them in a biscuit tin.   ☐

    He was wearing his favourite swirl badge.   ☐

    He'd saved for months to buy them.   ☐

    He was very excited.   ☐

3. **Find** and **copy two** things Bob did just before he left home.

    _____

    _____

4. Where was the show taking place?

    _____

5. *"A huge cheer filled the auditorium before it was replaced by an electric hush."*

    This means that the cheer was followed by the sound of ... Tick **one**.

    a loud bang   ☐   a buzzing lightbulb   ☐

    a squeaky microphone   ☐   an excited silence   ☐

6. How does Bob feel at the end of the story? Explain how you know.

    _____

    _____

Unit 2 Writing a story in the first person

In this unit children will:

- read part of a fantasy story about a dream coming true
- consider how the author constructs character by letting us know what they think and feel, as well as what they do
- think about the author's use of vocabulary to create atmosphere and paragraphs to organise ideas
- recognise the importance of telling a story in one tense and identify past tense verb forms
- plan, draft, edit and improve a first person fantasy story about a dream coming true.

Stage 1: Responding to the text

Activities:

- Establish prior knowledge.
  - Have any of the children read any of the *Bob, the Man on the Moon* books by Simon Bartram? If so, allow them to share their experiences.
  - Explain that Bob, and his trusty six-legged dog, Barry, work on the Moon. Bob shows space tourists around and puts on his own show for them. Bob definitely doesn't believe in aliens – but that doesn't mean they don't feature in all the stories.
  - *Think, pair, share:* What kinds of experiences do you think Bob might have on the Moon? Ask children to make notes of their ideas.
- Before reading the story, ensure the children understand the meaning of the more unusual words and phrases: *"revealed"*, *"lunar"*, *"emerge"*, *"realised"*, *"airing cupboard"*, *"trusty old video"*, *"auditorium"* and *"silhouette"*. Help the children remember the meanings of these words by putting them in contextualising sentences, e.g. *The alien slowly came out of the crater: it emerged bit by bit.*
- Introduce the text. Explain that the sentences in italics at the top of the page are there because this text is an extract (a short part) of a longer book, and the introduction is meant to give you information that you need to know in order to understand events in the extract.
- Ensure the children understand that the butterflies in Bob's stomach are a metaphor for how he is feeling. Ask the children if they have ever felt funny in the tummy when they were excited or apprehensive.
- Read and talk about the text.
  - Why was Bob so excited?
  - What is a 'live show'?
  - What kind of things might the Stupendous Alacazamo do in his show?
  - Why do you think the show starts with flashes and bangs?
- Ask children to answer the reading comprehension questions to ensure close reading of the text and good understanding. Talk about the way the author used the phrase *"electric hush"* in question 5. Ask the children what they think this means and discuss how these words describe the growing feeling of excitement. How might the audience feel this? (*Their hair standing up on their skin, goosebumps, butterflies in their tummies.*)
- Together, share answers to the questions and discuss the strategies children used to answer them.

Resources needed:

Shared copy of the text (PDF/IWB/visualiser)

Each child needs:

- a copy of the text
- a copy of the comprehension questions.

Stage 2: Analysing the text content

Activities:

- Ask children to read the text aloud to a response partner to revisit the text, develop fluency, ensure appropriate pronunciation of all words and to practise reading with good intonation and expression.
- Ask children to underline any new words or phrases. Take feedback and explain what these mean in context.

Resources needed:

Shared copy of the text (PDF/IWB/visualiser)

Each group needs:

- large paper

Each child needs:

- a copy of the text
- coloured pens/pencils.

Discussing the kind of story this is

- Ask children whether they think this text is:
  - an information text
  - a story about something that could happen
  - a fantasy story (where some things are like real life and other things are invented)
  - a traditional tale like *The Gingerbread Man*.
- Agree that it's a fantasy story. Ask children for ideas from the text which could not be true in real life (e.g. *Bob working on the Moon and coming home in the evening in his rocket*).

Discussing character

- Tell the children you want to find some information about Bob from the text. Model finding information about what he does (e.g. *tidies up space tourists' rubbish; flies a rocket*) and what he thinks or feels (e.g. *excited; always wanted to see the magic show*). Explain that some evidence is easy to find but other evidence you have to think about. (E.g. *He worries about having forgotten to put on his vest. What does that tell us about him?*)
- Ask groups of children to use the large sheet of paper to draw a large outline of an astronaut.
  - Ask them to think about what they know about Bob from the text.
    - Around the outside of the figure, they should list things they know about Bob's clothes and appearance, as well as what he does.
    - Inside the figure, ask them to record what we know about the kinds of things Bob likes and about his feelings.
  - Give children time to look at each other's records and see if they generally agree. If they disagree, allow them to politely challenge members of the group.
  - Can children tell you where in the text they got their information?
- Ask them to consider what we *don't* know about Bob (e.g. *his age; what he looks like; whether he is married; whether he likes his job*, etc.).
  - Ask children whether any of the information we don't know about him is necessary to understand what's going on in this extract.
  - Remind children that this is an extract so some more information will probably be shared elsewhere in the longer text.

Discussing setting

- Ask children what kind of show Bob is going to see (*magic/illusion*). Ask them to think of their experience of watching magic/illusion shows either live or on TV. Where might you go to see a magic show?
- Talk about how an audience might be prepared for the show.
- Would it feel like the same show if it were to be performed:
  - in the school hall?
  - in a public swimming pool?
  - on a football pitch?
  - in a village hall?
  - in a theatre?

  Clarify that the performance may be the same, but the atmosphere would be different in different settings.

- *Think pair, share:* Underline all the information we have about the setting for the show (e.g. *name of the Glitterball Theatre;* "grand, pillared entrance"; "lights dimmed"; "heavy, velvet curtains"; "stage").
  - In pairs, ask children to draw a quick sketch of the theatre and auditorium, labelling all the parts they can.
  - Talk about *why* we are given so much information about the setting for the show (e.g. *so that we understand the atmosphere and drama of the event*). Ask the children how they would describe the venue in their own words. How might they feel if they went somewhere so splendid?

Stage 3: Analysing the text structure and language 📖

Activities:

- Ask children to read the text aloud to a different response partner to revisit the text, develop fluency, ensure appropriate pronunciation of all words and to practise reading with good intonation and expression.

Discussing paragraphs

- What do children know about why and when we use paragraphs in stories? Clarify that paragraphs are usually organised around a theme, e.g.
  - a section of a story
  - an action, a period of time or event – paragraphs often begin with an adverb or adverbial phrase which tells us where or when the action takes place.
- In pairs, ask children to circle *one* adverb (or adverbial phase) at the beginning of a paragraph that indicates:
  - *where* action is taking place (e.g. *"At home"; "Having landed back at the Lunar Hill launch-pad"; "The streets outside …"*)
  - *when* action is taking place (e.g. *"It was almost time"*).
- Model summarising information from the first two paragraphs, e.g.
  - *paragraph 1: he hurried home from the Moon so he could go to the Stupendous Alacazamo's show*
  - *paragraph 2: he landed and quickly changed into Earth clothes.*
- Now ask the children in their pairs to use sticky notes to summarise the events from the other paragraphs. They should write the paragraph number on the sticky note, e.g.
  - *paragraph 3: he got ready and ate a sandwich*
  - *paragraph 4: Bob speaks*
  - *paragraph 5: he found his tickets*
  - *paragraph 6: he speaks to Barry*
  - *paragraph 7: he gets ready to go to the show*
  - *paragraph 8: everyone was going to the show; Bob arrives at the theatre*
  - *paragraph 9: the show began with a flash and a bang*
  - *paragraph 10: Bob saw the Stupendous Alacazamo*
- Hand out sheets of A4 paper, numbered 3–10, and ask children to put their sticky notes on the relevant paragraph number.
- Look together at the range of ideas for each paragraph and agree the best summary.
- Remind children that this is an extract from a longer book so the author didn't write it as a complete story leading up to an ending.

Resources needed:

Shared copy of the text (PDF/IWB/visualiser)

Each pair needs:

- an enlarged copy of the text
- sticky notes (3″/7.5 cm square – the purpose being to restrict the amount of writing space available)
- A4 paper

Each child needs:

- the copy of the text they have previously highlighted
- different coloured highlighters/pens/pencils.

Looking at vocabulary

- Model finding examples of each word class described below before asking children to work in pairs to find them.
- *Think, pair, share:* Ask children to use a colour to underline all of the words and phrases in the first three paragraphs that tell you Bob was in a hurry to get to the performance (e.g. *"quickly"*, *"quickly popped"*, *"super-fast flash"*, *"shoved"*, *"speedy"*, *"wolfed"*).
- Read the paragraphs aloud to the children, omitting the adjectives and adverbs and replacing the verbs with more general verbs (e.g. *"he quickly popped"/went*; *"he shoved on"/he put on*; *"he wolfed down"/he ate*). Point out that most of these words are descriptive verbs (e.g. *"popped"*, *"shoved"*, *"wolfed"*) or adverbs (e.g. *"quickly"*), although some are adjectives too (e.g. *"speedy"*, *"super-fast"*).
- Discuss the impact of the author's original language choices (e.g. *builds excitement and gives a very clear picture of how the character is behaving and what he is doing*).
- Now ask the children to use a different colour to underline all the information in the whole text that tells us that Bob and everyone else in the town is excited (e.g. *"so excited he could hardly fly his rocket straight"*; *"buzzing"*; *"an electric hush"*; *"butterflies began to swirl around Bob's tummy"*; *"dream come true"*; *"In front of his very eyes …"*; *"at last …"*). Can children identify adjectives in these phrases (e.g. *"buzzing"*, *"electric"*, *"very"*)?
- Talk about why the author chose to give us so much information about how excited Bob was (e.g. *he's using words to create the kind of excitement that the Stupendous Alacazamo creates with flashes and bangs in the theatre*).
- In a third colour, ask the children to find adjectives that describe what it was like in the theatre (e.g. *"grand"*, *"pillared"*, *"beautiful"*, *"heavy, velvet"*). Discuss the impact of the adjectives in the expanded noun phrases.

Looking at tense

- Ask children to tell you which tense the story is written in. (*Past.*)
  - Can they tell you how they know it's the past tense? Expect answers such as:
    - *stories are usually written in the past tense*
    - *there are lots of past tense verbs* (check children understand it's only the verb forms that are in the past tense).
  - In pairs, ask children to reread the first three paragraphs and find:
    - five past tense verb forms ending in -ed (e.g. *"wanted"*, *"landed"*, *"popped"*, *"shoved"*, *"cycled"*, *"realised"*, *"wolfed"*, *"selected"*, *"saved"*)
    - five past tense verb forms which don't end in -ed (e.g. *"was"*, *"didn't"*, *"could have been"*, *"had"*, *"would"*, *"dug"*, *"were"*).
- Discuss how confusing it would be for the reader if the tense kept changing. Agree that it's easier to follow the sequence of events if the story is just told in the past tense.

Looking at punctuation

- In pairs, ask children to highlight all the apostrophes they can find. Then ask them to list the words containing apostrophes in two sets:
  - apostrophes showing ownership: (*tourists'*, *Alacazamo's*, *Bob's*, *theatre's*)
  - apostrophes showing missing *letters*: (*didn't*, *o'clock*, *wasn't*, *hadn't*, *He'd*). Ensure the children can see the hidden verb in *"He'd"* (*he had*).
    - Clarify any misconceptions.
- Ask children to highlight one question mark and five exclamation marks.
  - Discuss why the author used this punctuation instead of full stops (e.g. *to mark a question; to build excitement and identify the way people said the words*).

Stage 4: Planning to write: Writing a story in the first person

Activities:

- Ask children to read the text aloud to a response partner while thinking how paragraphs and punctuation help the reader to read with fluency and expression.

Thinking about story ideas

- Tell the children they're going to write their own fantasy story about one of their dreams coming true. It doesn't have to be a true dream, but they are going to write it as if it were happening to them, using the pronouns *I, me*, etc.
- Together, brainstorm some different scenarios for fantasy stories in which dreams come true (e.g. *they could involve magic or magical creatures; they could take place in a different world*).
- In groups, ask children to brainstorm more ideas or discuss further the ones you recorded.
- Once groups have thought of a range of ideas, allow them time to select one, then ask them to role-play their idea, exploring a sequence of events. They might want to role-play it several times, swapping characters each time, so they have a coherent story at the end of the session.

Planning in pairs

- Distribute the writing framework.
- Model planning one of the story ideas you recorded earlier, demonstrating how to use the writing framework. Remind the children that the story will be told by them as if it had happened.
  - Remind children that this isn't their whole story and the boxes are for them to write and draw a brief summary for each phase of the story.
  - Explain that the words in the stars are adverbs of time and place. Children don't have to use all of them, but tell them that at least two of their paragraphs should begin with an adverb of time or place.
- Working in pairs, the children should add as much detail as is useful to their plans.
- Model improving the plan you made, adding in adverbs and adjectives.
- Tell your story in the first person, using the pronoun *I*.
- Remind children that they will need to tell their stories as if they had been there.
- Give each child the opportunity to 'talk like a writer' to a different response partner to say how they think the story will develop and to receive peer feedback.
- Ask the children to say what they think their new stories should include.
- Clarify and amend the success criteria (online at My Rising Stars) if appropriate.

Resources needed:

Shared copy of the text (PDF/IWB/visualiser)

The success criteria

Each group of children needs:
- large paper

Each child needs:
- the copy of the text they have previously highlighted and annotated
- marker pens/coloured pencils
- the writing framework from page 27 (some children may benefit from this being enlarged to A3).

Stage 5: Writing

Activities:

- Remind the children that they are going to write a fantasy story about one of their dreams coming true.
- Model turning your plan into the story. Ensure you use the features in the success criteria including the use of pronouns such as *I, me, mine, myself*, the past tense

Resources needed:

The success criteria

Each child needs:
- the copy of the text they have previously highlighted and annotated
- the completed writing framework.

(including the past progressive tense where appropriate), adverbs starting paragraphs to show change of time or place, description of the setting, verbs to add excitement.

- Give children a few minutes to 'talk like a writer' and tell another response partner the story as they plan to write it. If it helps, ask them to use a polite 'writer's voice'. Remind them to use their plan and not to invent another story as they go along.
- Let response partners give some brief feedback before children swap roles.
- Tell children your expectations about how much space each part of the story will take up on the page, e.g.
  - o introduction: 2–3 lines
  - o problem: 4–5 lines
  - o action: 4–5 lines
  - o outcome: 3–4 lines
  - o ending: 2–3 lines.

  (Amend these line numbers for your class and the amount of time they have to write.)
- Remind children they can compose and rehearse sentences inside their head or in a low whisper before they begin to write them.
- Read aloud the success criteria (online at My Rising Stars).
- Let the children write. Break up the writing process. Talk about the focus for each paragraph and quickly model a sentence or idea that the children could try out in their writing.
- Five minutes before the end of the stage, ask all children to stop writing and read their story aloud to themselves. If they find errors, missing words or words they can improve, they should use this opportunity to make changes.

Stage 6: Improving, editing, reviewing and sharing the writing ✏️

Activities:

- Revisit together the success criteria (online at My Rising Stars).
- Model the process below using your work as an example. The children can give you feedback on each step of the process. After you model a step, the children should have a go with their partner at editing their own work.
- Ask children to reread their texts three times with their response partner:

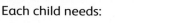

Resources needed:

Each child needs:
- the success criteria
- their writing/completed writing framework
- different coloured highlighters/pens.

  - o First read through: Children read their partner's text out loud to them. The child who wrote the text listens to check that their writing makes sense, listens out for obvious errors and checks the text follows their plan. Children then swap roles.
  - o Second read through: Children read their partner's text and highlight the success criteria they have met. They suggest three places where their partner could improve their work (to achieve or further improve on the success criteria).
  - o Third read through: Children proofread their partner's text together with them. They check for errors in punctuation and spelling and correct these as necessary. You should give input at this stage if needed.

Lessons from writing

Prior to the session, identify errors that were commonly made. Write sample sentences that need to be corrected and ask the children to help you to fix them. These could include:

- generic descriptions, e.g. *The planet was grey and brown. There were some blue plants and there were some red flowers. She saw some mountains in the distance. They were brown.* Challenge children to include some other descriptive adjectives (e.g. *huge, tiny, fat, enormous*) as well as some evaluative adjectives (e.g. *pretty, surprising, interesting, amazing, disgusting*) to create a more powerful image for the reader.

- mixed tenses, e.g. *Anya and Samir crept forwards. "Look!" hissed Samir. "I can see it!" replied Anya.*

  They run away as fast as they can. They want to escape the dragon before it wakes up.

Can children identify where the error creeps in in this piece of writing? Dialogue is usually in the present tense and it's easy to continue to write in the present tense. Ask children to correct the incorrect tenses.

Improving the writing

- **After the stories have been marked:** give the children time to read through your comments, to look at the success criteria and to implement any changes suggested. This should not involve the children rewriting the entire story – just those parts that you would like them to revisit to practise/improve their writing.

Share

Sometimes, children write stories to practise writing stories. Other times, there is a planned reason or an audience. If you want children to share their writing:

- they can word-process it; however, this should be regarded simply as a keyboarding activity not as another opportunity to improve the text – the rewritten text should be used for a specific audience or display
- they could polish their ideas in their groups and create a short play to share with the class
- use a multimedia presentation package; ask children to create their best drawings of each of the stages in their story, then read their story aloud, accompanied by the illustrations, to make their own e-books – you could publish these on the school website.

Unit 2: Writing a story in the first person

Name: **Class:**   **Date:**

Use the boxes below to plan your fantasy story about dreams coming true. Use the adverbs on this page for ideas of how to begin your paragraphs and write your chosen adverbs in the smaller boxes. In your story, at least two paragraphs should begin with an adverb.

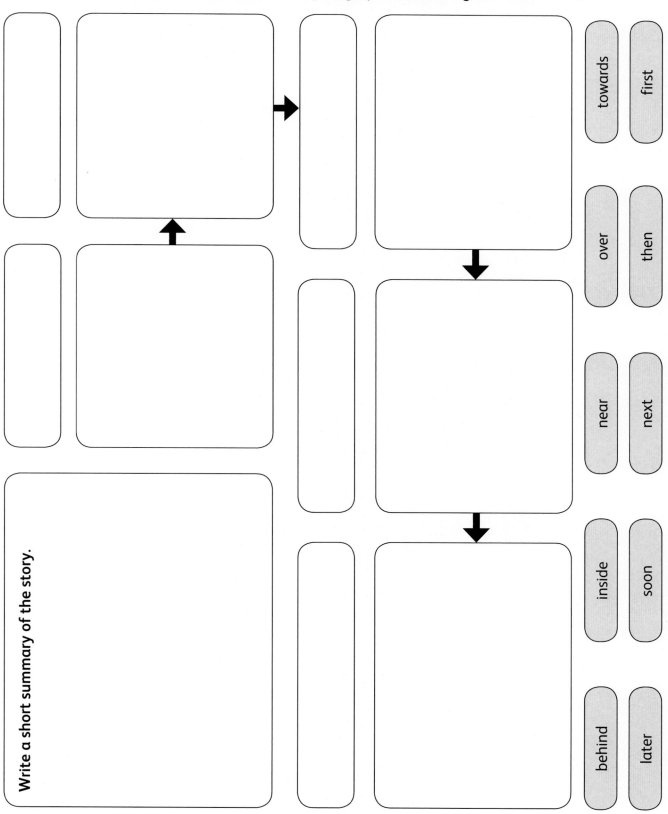

Write a short summary of the story.

towards   first

over   then

near   next

inside   soon

behind   later

Unit 2: Moderating writing: Writing a story in the first person

Name: Date:

	Contents	Text structure and organisation	Sentence structure	Vocabulary and descriptions	Punctuation	Spelling and handwriting
Working **at greater depth within** the expected standard	Characters and settings are consistent and convincing.	Paragraphs introduce a change of speaker, time, place or action.	The story is written consistently in the past tense, except in dialogue.	More sophisticated vocabulary is used to create atmosphere.	Inverted commas and other punctuation are used in dialogue.	Spelling changes needed to add vowel suffixes are often accurate.
	At least one additional detail is included to help the reader to engage with the text.	The story has a satisfying shape leading to an exciting action, outcome and ending.	Appropriate choice of pronouns is used to avoid repetition.	Noun phrases may be extended with prepositional phrases.	Apostrophes are only used in appropriate contexts.	In handwriting, most letters are appropriately joined or word-processing speed is developing and does not impede thought processes.
Working **at** the expected standard	The fantasy story is about dreams coming true.	Paragraphs are used to distinguish different sections in the story.	Some paragraphs begin with an adverb to show a change of time or place.	Some thoughtful choices of technical vocabulary (linked to the Moon or aliens) is included.	Apostrophes are used to show possession (singular).	A range of prefixes and suffixes is used.
	The story is told in the first person.		Use of pronouns such as I, me, mine, myself, we, us, ours, ourselves is shown.		Commas are used to separate items in lists.	Taught spellings from the Year 3/4 word list are correct.
	Some attempt is made to develop character and setting using descriptive verbs (e.g. strode) or adverbs (e.g. confidently).	The story leads towards a single interesting event.	Conjunctions, adverbs and prepositions are used to show when, where and why events occur.	Descriptive verbs make the action fast paced.	End of sentence punctuation (.?!) is generally accurate.	Some letters are joined using diagonal or horizontal strokes.
						Letters and spaces are in proportion to each other.
Working **towards** the expected standard	The story follows the plan.	Ideas are grouped and sequenced appropriately.	At least three different conjunctions are used correctly.	Some expanded noun phrases are used.	End of sentence punctuation (.?!) is often accurate.	Spelling errors are phonetically decodable.
	The story is about dreams coming true.		Most of the story is in the past tense.	Some fantasy-related vocabulary is used.	Apostrophes are used for contractions (missing letters).	Spaces between letters and words allow for good legibility.

Frankie vs. the Pirate Pillagers

Frank Lampard

> *Frankie won a battered old football on a strange stall at the funfair. He and his friends Charlie and Louise, and his dog Max, stopped to play with the ball in the park on their way home.*

"There!" said Charlie, pointing to a climbing frame shaped like a model ship. He jogged over and stood in front of it. "The ship's the goal."

Frankie booted the ball high into the air. Max streaked after it. It tangled in his feet, and he tumbled over the top.

"Pass it!" called Frankie.

Max managed to nose the ball to Louise. She dribbled the ball in and out of the swings, then sent a curling shot towards the top corner of the goal. Charlie dived and just got his fingertips to the ball.

"Nothing gets past me!" said Charlie.

We'll see about that … thought Frankie. He fetched the ball and passed it to Louise. She looked up, ready to shoot, then stepped over the ball and flicked it up with her heel. Frankie was ready. He brought his foot round and connected with a perfect volley. The ball screamed towards the goal. Charlie leapt sideways, gloves splayed, but the ball passed beneath his outstretched hands. Frankie slid on to his knees thinking his mum would kill him when she saw the grass stains.

"SUPERGOA …"

The shout trailed off in Frankie's throat.

The ball had vanished, and so had the model ship. Max growled quietly. Frankie stood up, his heart thumping. He couldn't believe what was before his eyes.

Where the goal had been just a second ago was a swirl of light like nothing he'd ever seen. Colours flashed and spun in a disc shape, three metres across. He looked at Louise. Her jaw had dropped open.

Charlie picked himself up, bashing the ground with his fist. He still hadn't seen the spinning circle of light behind him. "I was so close!" he said.

"Er, Charlie," said Louise. "You might want to turn around." He did as she told him, then leapt backwards. "Holy moly! What is that thing?"

Frankie and Louise joined Charlie's side. The lights shifted and shimmered like oil on water.

"I have no idea!" said Frankie. "But it must be linked to the ball."

Name: Class: Date:

1. What did Frankie and his friends decide to use as a goal?

    _____

2. (a) Which of the children is playing in goal? Circle **one**.

        Frankie   Max   Louise   Charlie

    (b) Which member of Frankie's team is not a child? Circle **one**.

        Frankie   Max   Louise   Charlie

3. Find and copy **one** word from the text which shows the shot that Frankie kicked was going fast towards the goal.

    _____

4. *"SUPERGOA …"*

    Why do you think Frankie didn't finish the word?

    _____

5. Why did Louise say Charlie should turn round?

    _____

6. Tick **three** things that were true about the swirl of light.

    It made a humming noise.   ☐

    Colours flashed across it.   ☐

    It spun in a disc shape.   ☐

    It was made of oil.   ☐

    It was three metres across.   ☐

Unit 3 Continuing a fantasy story

In this unit children will:

- read the beginning of a fantasy story
- recognise how conjunctions and adverbs support the use of paragraphs in guiding the reader through the story
- identify features of the setting and characters through what we are told and what we can infer
- consider how and why the author uses dialogue
- plan, draft, edit and improve a continuation of the story, using information and description from the model text.

Stage 1: Responding to the text

Activities:

- Establish prior knowledge.
  - Have any of the children read any of the *Frankie's Magic Football* stories? If so, allow them to share their experiences.
  - Have any of them heard of the author Frank Lampard? He is a professional footballer who played for England and Chelsea.

Resources needed:

Shared copy of the text (PDF/IWB/visualiser)

Each child needs:

- a copy of the text
- a copy of the comprehension questions.

- Explain that this is the first book in the series. Frankie is football mad. He wins an old, battered football at a fair, only to discover that the football is magic.
- Ask children to think of different ways in which a football could be magic (e.g. *it could change shape; it could stick to the end of your shoe; it could change the person who kicks it; it could change direction in mid-air*).
- *Think, pair, share:* Ask children to choose two of the ideas the class suggested, and to talk briefly to each other about which idea they think would make for the most interesting story and why.
- Introduce the text. Explain that the sentences in italics at the top of the page are there because this text is an extract (a short part) of a longer book, and the introduction is meant to give you information that you need to know in order to understand events in the extract.
- Before reading the story, ensure the children understand the meaning of the more unusual words and phrases and footballing vocabulary: "*shimmered*", "*booted*", "*streaked*" and "*dribbled*". Help the children remember the meanings of these words by putting them in contextualising sentences, e.g. *The candlelight flickered and shimmered in the darkness.*
- Read and talk about the text.
  - Do the children think Frankie's right in thinking the spinning disc is linked to the ball?
  - What do they think the children will do next?
  - Do they think this is a real-life story or a fantasy story (where either invented things happen in the real world, or real things happen in an invented world)?
- Ask the children to answer the reading comprehension questions to ensure close reading of the text and good understanding.
- Together, share answers to the questions and discuss the strategies children used to answer them. Discuss question 4 where the author doesn't actually tell us about what's happened, but still manages to show us that something odd has happened.

Stage 2: Analysing the text content

Activities:

- Ask children to read the text aloud to a response partner to revisit the text, develop fluency, ensure appropriate pronunciation of all words and to practise reading with good intonation and expression.
- Ask children to underline any new words or phrases. Take feedback and explain what these mean in context.

Discussing plot

- Remind children of the most common 'shape' of a story:
  - Introduction – we're given background information
  - Problem – we're introduced to the reason for the events in the story
  - Action – the main characters do or think something
  - Outcome – what happens after the action
  - Ending – tidies up all the ideas.
- *Think, pair, share:* Which part (or parts) of a story do we have in this extract? (E.g. *introduction and problem.*)
- Ask them to explain how they came to their decision (e.g. *we know who the characters are and where they got the ball (introduction) and we know that they have made/found a huge swirl of light, but lost their ball (problem)*).

Discussing setting and character

- Check that children are familiar with the word 'setting' (*meaning the place, time, weather, etc. in which a story is set*).
- Organise children into small groups. Ask them what they think the setting:
  - for the first part of the story was (*funfair*)
  - for this part of the story is (*playground*).
- Model identifying and underlining some details about the setting for this story (e.g. *in the introduction: strange stall at the funfair … the park*).
  - Ask them to underline as many details as they can about the setting (*"climbing frame shaped like a model ship", "swings"*).
  - Discuss why there are comparatively few details about the setting (e.g. *the plot is more important; we all know what playgrounds look like so we can image the rest; this setting is not important in the story – it's only a place for the ball to open the portal into an adventure*).
- Ask children to use a different colour and underline everything we know about the characters. Model finding and inferring information (e.g. *the characters are old enough to be out without their parents but young enough to play in the park*).
  - *Frankie rises to a challenge; he helps Louise to trick Charlie*
  - *Charlie plays in goal and thinks he's a good goalie*
  - *Louise is good at kicking and dribbling the ball; she helps Frankie to trick Charlie*
  - *Max is a little dog who can chase a ball and nose the ball to pass it.*
    - Discuss why there are so few details about the characters (e.g. *there might be more elsewhere in the book like in the introduction (there aren't); the kinds of people they are doesn't matter in the story – the characters of the children show in what they do and say, not in descriptions of them*).

Resources needed:

Shared copy of the text (PDF/IWB/ visualiser)

Each group needs:

- an enlarged copy of the text

Each child needs:

- a copy of the text
- different coloured highlighters/pens/pencils.

Stage 3: Analysing the text structure and language

Resources needed:

Shared copy of the text (PDF/IWB/visualiser)

Each pair needs:
- an enlarged copy of the text

Each child needs:
- the copy of the text they have previously highlighted and annotated
- different coloured highlighters/pens/pencils.

Activities:

Discussing dialogue

- Ask children what to look for as you scan a text to see where people speak (e.g. *inverted commas; clauses like "he said"; new paragraphs to show where a different person speaks*).
- Ask them to underline all dialogue to check that these conditions are met.
- Ask them how to find the words the character actually says (e.g. *they're in between the inverted commas*).
- In pairs, ask children to use different colours to highlight the words spoken by each character.
- Ask children to find somewhere in the text where:
  - there is no new paragraph between two bits of dialogue (e.g. *paragraph 2 has some description between different parts of the same speech*)
  - a word other than 'said' is used (e.g. *"called" in paragraph 4*)
  - the author shows thought instead of speech (e.g. *"We'll see about that" in paragraph 7 which is shown in italics, not inverted commas because the words are not said aloud*)
  - a piece of dialogue which doesn't have a *"he said"* clause (e.g. *"SUPERGOA ..."*)
    - Where are we given the information we need to infer who said the words? (*The next paragraph: The "shout trailed off ..."*)
    - Clarify that having one or two of these unattributed pieces of dialogue is sometimes OK, but a string of them isn't helpful for the reader.
  - a speech starts within a paragraph (e.g. *paragraph 12 where Charlie says "I was so close!"*).
    - Point out that the rest of the paragraph has already directed the reader's attention to a particular character and that character is speaking, so we don't need a new paragraph because it's not a new speaker.
- Talk about the purpose of dialogue in the story (e.g. *it lets us know what characters are thinking; it helps us to see how the characters feel about each other; it adds new information to the story*). Each time the children suggest an idea, model finding an example of how some of the dialogue in the story fulfils that function.
- Ask children why they think writers take time to mark dialogue very carefully. Agree that the aim is to make it easy for the reader to know what's going on.

Discussing description

- Challenge children to work in pairs and find:
  - five noun phrases which include an adjective (e.g. *"a battered old football"; "a strange stall"; "a model ship"; "a curling shot"; "the top corner"; "a perfect volley"; "a disc shape"; "the spinning circle"*)
  - five descriptive verbs (e.g. *"booted", "streaked", "to nose", "tangled", "tumbled", "dribbled", "flicked", "connected", "screamed", "leapt", "slid", "bashing", "vanished", "flashed", "spun", "shifted", "shimmered"*)
  - an adverb explaining how a verb was done (e.g. *"quietly"*).
- Make links with the work you did during Stage 2 (above) on understanding that the emphasis in the text is on action – exemplified by all the descriptive verbs – rather than on adjectives or adverbs.

Discussing time, place and cause

- Check whether the children remember the kind of information that conjunctions, adverbs and prepositions give us:
  - the order of events (*when they happened*)
  - the place of the events (*where they happened*)
  - the cause of events (*why they happened*).

- Model finding examples of each word class.
- Ask children to work in pairs to underline:
  - subordinating conjunctions introducing a clause which gives additional information (e.g. *when, so, and, but*)
  - adverbs (e.g. *over, then, around*)
  - prepositions, which are always followed by a pronoun or a noun phrase, and show us where or when one thing is in relation to another (e.g. *before, into, in front, about, over, with*).
- Discuss the fact that, in this text, there are few adverbs at the beginning of paragraphs, so we need to use the order of the paragraphs to understand the order of events.

Looking at punctuation

- Remind children what an apostrophe looks like and what it signals (e.g. *ownership/missing letters*).
- In pairs, ask children to highlight all the apostrophes they can find. Then ask them to list the words containing apostrophes in two sets:
  - apostrophes showing ownership (*Frankie's*)
  - apostrophe showing missing letters (*ship's, we'll, couldn't, he'd, hadn't*).
    - Clarify any misconceptions.
    - Check that all children are able to expand the contracted forms and can find the hidden verbs in *he is, we will, he had*.
- Ask children to highlight five exclamation marks.
  - Discuss why the author used this punctuation instead of full stops.

Stage 4: Planning to write: Continuing a fantasy story

Activities:

- Ask children to read the text aloud to a response partner while thinking how paragraphs and punctuation help the reader to read with fluency and expression.

Thinking about story ideas

- Tell the children that you want them to continue the story about Frankie, Charlie, Max and Louise.
- Together, discuss where the ball might have gone (e.g. *another world, the same world in a different time, the same world in a different place*).
- *Think, pair, share:*
  - Will Frankie and his friends shrug and go home, or go through the spinning disc to retrieve the ball? (*This is the beginning of the story. They've got to go and retrieve the ball.*)
  - Which clues in the text might help us to think about where the ball might have gone? (E.g. *The goal was a model ship which has disappeared.*)
- Choose one of the ideas children suggest and model sketching key features of the setting. Label your setting features using expanded noun phrases.
- In pairs, ask children to:
  - sketch the time or place the football might have gone to (children should make separate sketches)
  - label the sketches using adjectives to make expanded noun phrases.

Resources needed:

Shared copy of the text (PDF/IWB/visualiser)

The success criteria

Pairs of children need:
- paper for drawing

Each child needs:
- the copy of the text they have previously highlighted and annotated
- marker pens/coloured pencils
- the writing framework from page 38 (some children may benefit from this being enlarged to A3).

- Each child should now take their sketch and join another child to make a different pair. In their new pairs, ask children to:
  - discuss one child's sketch and consider actions that could occur there; encourage children to co-create a story
  - consider the other child's sketch and co-create a new story.
- Children should then join with their original pair and tell each other the stories they have created in the settings.

Planning in pairs

- Distribute the writing framework.
  - Model completing the writing framework by writing or drawing in the main boxes and using the boxes with dotted lines to record expanded noun phrases and descriptive verbs.
  - Remind children that the boxes are for them to write a brief summary for each phase of the story.
  - Encourage them to use the boxes beside the story boxes to record some key words from the sketch map to describe the setting or action.
- Working in pairs, the children should add as much detail as is useful to their plans.
- Give each child the opportunity to 'talk like a writer' to a different response partner to say how they think the story will develop and to receive peer feedback.
- Ask the children to say what they think their new stories should include.
- Clarify and amend the success criteria (online at My Rising Stars) if appropriate.

Stage 5: Writing

Activities:

- Remind the children that they are going to continue the story about Frankie, Charlie, Max and Louise.
- Model using your plan to write part of the story. Ensure you include examples of the success criteria including: descriptive verbs, expanded noun phrases, prepositions to show clearly where things are in relation to each other and dialogue that lets us know how characters are feeling and what they are thinking.

Resources needed:

The success criteria

Each child needs:

- the copy of the text they have previously highlighted
- the completed writing framework.

- Give children a few minutes to 'talk like a writer' and tell another response partner the story as they plan to write it. If it helps, ask them to use a polite 'writer's voice'. Remind them to use their plan and not to invent another story as they go along.
- Let response partners give some brief feedback before children swap roles.
- Tell children your expectations about how much space each part of the story will take up on the page, e.g.
  - introduction: 2–3 lines
  - problem: 4–5 lines
  - action: 4–5 lines
  - outcome: 3–4 lines
  - ending: 2–3 lines.

  (Amend these line numbers for your class and the amount of time they have to write.)
- Remind children they can compose and rehearse sentences inside their head or in a low whisper before they begin to write them.
- Read aloud the success criteria (online at My Rising Stars).
- Let the children write. Break up the writing process. Talk about the focus for each paragraph and quickly model a sentence or idea that the children could try out in their writing.
- Five minutes before the end of the stage, ask the children to stop writing and read their story aloud to themselves. If they find errors, missing words or words they can improve, they should use this opportunity to make changes.

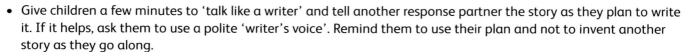

Stage 6: Improving, editing, reviewing and sharing the writing

Activities:

- Revisit together the success criteria (online at My Rising Stars).
- Model the process below using your work as an example. The children can give you feedback on each step of the process. After you model a step the children should have a go with their partner at editing their own work.

Resources needed:

Each child needs:

- the success criteria
- their writing/completed writing framework
- different coloured highlighters/pens/pencils.

- Ask children to reread their texts three times with their response partner:

  o First read through: Children read their partner's text out loud to them. The child who wrote the text listens to check that their writing makes sense, listens out for obvious errors and checks the text follows their plan. Children then swap roles.

  o Second read through: Children read their partner's text and highlight the success criteria they have met. They suggest three places where their partner could improve their work (to achieve or further improve on the success criteria).

  o Third read through: Children proofread their partner's text together with them. They check for errors in punctuation and spelling and correct these as necessary. You should give input at this stage if needed.

Lessons from writing

- Prior to the session, identify errors that were commonly made. Write sample sentences that need to be corrected and ask the children to help you to fix them. These could include:

  o not using descriptive verbs, e.g. *Max saw a pirate ship on the sea. Pirates were getting off into a little boat and coming closer. Max had seen his ball on the beach but he didn't want to go closer to the pirates.*

    ▪ Ask children to make the text much more interesting to read by exploring different verbs.

  o not laying out dialogue properly, e.g. *Let's play football said the pirate. Let's see how good you kids are. OK said Frankie. He drew some lines in the sand. This is our goal. Charlie is our goalie. The pirate went further down the beach. This is our goal, he said. Big Len is our goalie.*

    ▪ Challenge children to show you how to lay out the dialogue properly.

Improving the writing

- **After the stories have been marked:** give the children time to read through your comments, to look at the success criteria and to implement any changes suggested. This should not involve the children rewriting the entire story – just those parts that you would like them to revisit to practise/improve their writing.

Share

Sometimes, children write stories to practise writing stories. Other times, there is a planned reason or an audience. If you want children to share their writing:

- they can copy it out in presentation handwriting; however, this should be regarded simply as a handwriting activity not as another opportunity to improve the text – the rewritten text should be used for a specific audience or display
- create a display of *Frankie's Magic Football* stories showing artwork as well as well-presented stories
- let children make part of their stories into comic strips, using speech bubbles for dialogue
- teach children how to lay out playscripts and encourage them to rework their stories into plays.

Unit 3: Continuing a fantasy story

Name: **Class:**   **Date:**

Use the boxes in the middle to record the main ideas for each part of your story. Write down key words you could use to describe the setting and action in the boxes to the right of them.

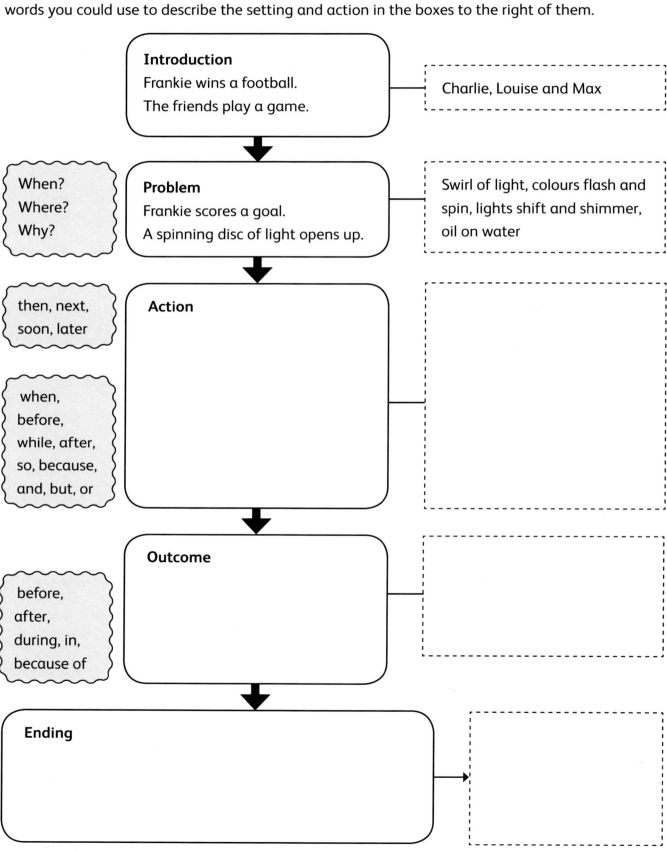

Introduction
Frankie wins a football.
The friends play a game.

Charlie, Louise and Max

When?
Where?
Why?

Problem
Frankie scores a goal.
A spinning disc of light opens up.

Swirl of light, colours flash and spin, lights shift and shimmer, oil on water

then, next, soon, later

Action

when, before, while, after, so, because, and, but, or

before, after, during, in, because of

Outcome

Ending

Name: Date:

	Contents	Text structure and organisation	Sentence structure	Vocabulary and descriptions	Punctuation	Spelling and handwriting
Working **at greater depth within** the expected standard	Characters and settings are consistent and convincing. At least one additional detail is included to help the reader to engage with the text.	Paragraphs introduce a change of speakers, time, place or action. The story has a satisfying shape leading to an exciting action, outcome and ending.	The story is consistently in the past tense, except in dialogue. Appropriate choice of pronouns is used to avoid repetition.	More sophisticated vocabulary is used to create atmosphere. Noun phrases may be extended with prepositional phrases.	Inverted commas and other punctuation are used in dialogue. Apostrophes are only used in appropriate contexts.	Spelling changes needed to add vowel suffixes are often accurate. In handwriting, most letters are appropriately joined or word-processing speed is developing and does not impede thought processes.
Working **at** the expected standard	A continuation of the story about Frankie's magic football is written. Some attempt is made to develop the characters of Frankie, Max and Louise and the fantasy setting.	Paragraphs are used to distinguish different sections in the story. The story leads towards a single interesting event.	Some paragraphs begin with an adverb to show a change of time or place. The text includes at least two different types of sentence. Prepositions are used to show how things are related in time (e.g. *in, on, at, since*) and space (e.g. *through, under, nearby*).	Some thoughtful choices of technical vocabulary (linked to football or to the vortex) is included. Descriptive verbs make the action fast paced.	Inverted commas and new lines for new speakers are used in dialogue. Apostrophes are used to show possession (singular). End of sentence punctuation (.?!) is generally accurate. Commas are used to separate items in lists.	A range of prefixes and suffixes is used. Taught spellings from the Year 3/4 word list are correct. Some letters are joined using diagonal or horizontal strokes. Letters and spaces are in proportion to each other.
Working **towards** the expected standard	The story follows the plan. The story includes a magic football.	Ideas are grouped and sequenced appropriately.	At least three different conjunctions are used correctly. Most of the story is in the past tense.	Some expanded noun phrases are used. Some football-related vocabulary is used.	End of sentence punctuation (.?!) is often accurate. Apostrophes are used for contractions (missing letters).	Spelling errors are phonetically decodable. Spaces between letters and words allow for good legibility.

Storm

Kevin Crossley-Holland

> *Annie Carter lives with her disabled parents in a remote cottage on the edge of a marsh. Her older sister, who is due to have a baby, has come to stay. Late one night, in the middle of a terrible storm, the baby decides to be born. They can't phone the doctor and they don't have a car. There's nothing for it but for Annie to walk into the nearby town of Waterslain and get help.*

When Mrs Carter opened the cottage door, the wind snatched it out of her hands and slammed the door against the wall.

"Blast!" said Mr Carter. "That's a rough old night!"

The four of them stood just inside the door, huddled together, staring out, getting used to the storm and the darkness.

There was a slice of moon well up in the sky. It seemed to be speeding behind grey lumpy clouds, running away from something that was chasing it. The Carters' little garden looked ashen and the marsh looked ashen and Mr Elins' fields looked ashen.

They all heard it then: the sound of hooves, galloping.

"Blast!" said Mr Carter. "Who can that be, then?"

"In this storm!" cried Annie's mother.

"At midnight," said Mr Carter.

Annie slipped one hand inside her mother's hand. The hooves drummed louder and louder, almost on top of them, and round the corner of the cottage galloped a horseman on a fine chestnut mare.

"Whoa!" shouted the rider when he saw Annie and her family standing at the cottage door.

"That's not Elkins, then," said Mr Carter, hauling himself in front of his wife and daughters. "That's not his horse." The horseman stopped just outside the pool of light streaming through the open door, and none of them recognised him. He was tall and unsmiling.

"That's a rough old night," Mr Carter called out.

The horseman nodded and said not a word.

"Are you going into Waterslain?"

"Waterslain?" said the horseman. "Not in particular."

"Blast!" said Mr Carter in a thoughtful kind of way.

"I could go," said the horseman in a dark voice, "if there was a need."

Then Annie's mother loosed her daughter's hand and stepped out into the storm and soon explained the need, and Mr Carter went out and asked the horseman his name. The wind gave a shriek and Annie was unable to catch his reply. "So you see," said Annie's mother, "there's no time to be lost."

"Come on up, Annie," said the horseman.

"It's all right," said Annie, shaking her head.

"I'll take you," said the horseman.

"You'll be fine," said Mrs Carter.

"I can walk," insisted Annie.

But the horseman quickly bent down and put a hand under one of Annie's shoulders and swung her up onto the saddle in front of him as if she were as light as thistledown. Then he raised one hand and spurred his horse. Mr and Mrs Carter stood and watched as Annie turned away the full white moon of her face, and then she and the horseman were swallowed up in the stormy darkness.

Name: **Class:**   **Date:**

1. Why did the family stand near the door?

    _____

2. *"The Carters' little garden looked ashen ..."*

    In this sentence, tick **one** word or phrase that *ashen* is closest to in meaning.

    on fire   ☐   pale and grey   ☐

    covered in ash   ☐   colourful   ☐

3. Which sound made Annie want to hold her mother's hand?

    _____

4. Tick **three** things we know about the horseman.

    He didn't smile.   ☐

    He had chestnut hair.   ☐

    He was tall.   ☐

    He was a neighbour.   ☐

    He was a stranger.   ☐

5. What do you think Annie's mother said to the horseman?

    _____

6. Where was Annie going at the end of this extract?

    _____

Unit 4 Writing a story with a strong setting

In this unit children will:

- read part of a story with a strong setting
- explore how the author uses setting to create atmosphere and evoke all five senses
- identify what we're told and what we can infer about a character, including through dialogue
- consider using both noun phrases and descriptive verbs for description
  - clarify and discuss the role of paragraphs in helping us to understand the sequence of events
  - plan, draft, edit and improve a story with a strong setting about a rescue during a storm.

Stage 1: Responding to the text

Activities:

- Establish prior knowledge.
  - Have any of the children been outside in a storm? Or watched storms from inside a house? Ask them to:
    - jot down 5–10 words or phrases they think of when they think about a storm (e.g. *wind, rain, thunder, lightning, gale, hurricane, slam, break, rumble, flash, shivering, cold, boughs bending, roof collapsing, flooding, hail, deluge, drench, force, downpour, tossed, calm, lull, blow, fury, rescue, danger*)
    - write on the divided A4 paper (see the box to the right), using the initial letter of each word or phrase to write it in the relevant box (e.g. *wind* goes in *u, v, w*; *rain* goes under *q, r*, etc.)
    - share and swap words with three or four other children to expand their storm vocabulary.
- Ask each child to choose the one or two words they are most proud of so that together you create your class 'storm' thesaurus. Encourage children to copy down additional words into their own list of storm words.
- Introduce the text. Explain that the sentences in italics at the top of the page are there because this text is an extract (a short part) of a longer book and the introduction is meant to give you information that you need to know in order to understand events in the extract.
- Before reading the story, ensure the children understand the meaning of the more unusual words and phrases: *"mare", "marsh", "spurred", "horseman", "thistledown"* and *"ashen"*. Help the children remember the meanings of these words by putting them in contextualising sentences, e.g. *The winding road made everyone nervous; our faces were grey and ashen.*
- Read and talk about the text.
  - Do children think Annie's parents were wise letting her go with a stranger? (*Reassure them that Annie is quite safe!*)
  - Why did Annie have to go into Waterslain without her family?
  - Who do children think the horseman might be?
- Ask the children to answer the reading comprehension questions to ensure close reading of the text and good understanding.
- Together, share answers to the questions and discuss the strategies children used to answer them. Discuss question 5 with the children. Model using clues from the text to help you decide what the mother is likely to say to the horseman.

Resources needed:

Shared copy of the text (PDF/IWB/visualiser)

Each child needs:

- A4 paper divided into 12 equal sections, each section labelled with two letters of the alphabet (until the final two sections labelled: *u, v, w* and *x, y, z*)
- a copy of the text
- a copy of the comprehension questions.

Stage 2: Analysing the text content

Activities:

- Ask children to read the text aloud to a response partner to revisit the text, develop fluency, ensure appropriate pronunciation of all words and to practise reading with good intonation and expression.
- Ask children to underline any new words or phrases. Take feedback and explain what these mean in context.

Resources needed:

Shared copy of the text (PDF/IWB/ visualiser)

Each group needs:

- an enlarged copy of the text
- large paper.

Each child needs:

- a copy of the text
- coloured highlighters/pens/pencils.

Discussing setting

- Ask children what they think the word 'setting' means. Clarify that it can mean the weather as well as the time and place. Model finding some examples of the setting as weather, time and place.
- In groups, ask children to read the text and find out what they can about:
    - the place (e.g. *remote cottage, edge of marsh, cottage doorway, ashen garden*)
    - the time (e.g. *late one night*)
    - the weather (e.g. *terrible storm; wind snatches door; rough old night; darkness; slice of moon running away; grey lumpy clouds*).
- Talk about why, in this extract, the author gives more information about the weather than about the place (e.g. *perhaps the place was described in an earlier chapter; the stormy atmosphere is important at this point in the story*).
- Ask children to underline all references to the storm.
- Discuss why there are references to the storm throughout the text. Agree that the writer doesn't want the reader to forget that it's a stormy night.
- In their groups, invite children to talk about the kinds of events that might happen in a story with this type of setting.
    - Ask if it is more likely to be a happy, busy story or a scary story.
    - Discuss children's answers. Ask them to justify their opinions.

Discussing senses

- Remind children that we have five senses: sight, smell, taste, hearing and touch.
- Identify some of the stronger imagery in the text (e.g. *"the wind snatched the door"; "the hooves drummed louder and louder"; "a slice of moon … behind grey lumpy clouds, running away from something that was chasing it"; "the pool of light streaming"; "the wind gave a shriek"; "the full white moon of her face … swallowed up in the stormy darkness"*). Explain to the children what you 'see' in your head as you read each image.
- Ask groups to write the name of each of the senses on a large sheet of paper and then to read the text together looking for evidence of each of the senses. Together, discuss which senses they would use for the imagery you have discussed. They should record words or phrases beside the headings on their large sheet of paper, e.g.
    - sight: *slice of moon behind grey lumpy clouds; ashen garden; tall unsmiling horseman; pool of light; full white moon of Annie's face*
    - sound: *door slamming on wall, hooves galloping, conversation, shrieking wind*
    - touch: *huddling together, slipping hand into mother's, horseman lifting Annie, spurring on his horse.*
- Talk about the impact on the reader of having information about so many senses. In most stories, we just learn about what is seen, not what is heard and felt. (E.g. *It makes it feel more real; it makes you think you're there.*)

Discussing character

- Ask children who they think is the main character in this extract. (*Annie.*)
- Ask children to work in pairs to make a table.
  - One child should record what we're told about Annie. The other should record what we can work out from what we're told about Annie.
  - Model this process for one of the examples, e.g.

We're told	We can work out
Anne must walk into Waterslain to get help.	*She must be old enough to walk there alone.*
She stood with her family looking at the storm.	*She didn't much want to go out.*
She didn't know the horseman, nor could she hear his name.	*She was probably frightened.*
Her face was a full white moon.	*She was probably scared.*

- Discuss why it's important that we think about what we can work out as well as what we're told (e.g. *it gives us a better understanding of the character and it allows the author to give us key details without telling us everything*).

Stage 3: Analysing the text structure and language

Activities:

Discussing dialogue

- Ask children what to look for as you scan a text to see where people speak (e.g. *inverted commas; clauses like "he said"; new paragraphs to show where a different person speaks*).
- Ask them how to find the words the character actually says (e.g. *they're in between the inverted commas*).
- Which characters' words do we 'hear' in this text? (*Mr Carter; the horseman; Annie's mother; Annie.*)
  - In pairs, ask children to use different colours to highlight the words spoken by each character.
- Ask children to find somewhere in the text where a word other than *said* is used (e.g. *"asked", "shouted", "called out"*).
- Ask children why they think writers take time to mark dialogue very carefully. Agree that the aim is to make it easy for the reader to know what's going on.

Resources needed:

Shared copy of the text (PDF/IWB/visualiser)

Each pair needs:

- an enlarged copy of the text
- different coloured highlighters/pens/pencils.

Each child needs:

- the copy of the text they have previously highlighted
- their 'storm' thesaurus from Stage 1
- marker pens/coloured pencils.

Discussing description

- Challenge children to work in pairs and find:
  - five noun phrases which include an adjective (e.g. *"grey lumpy clouds"; "the Carters' little garden"; "fine chestnut mare"; "the cottage door"; "a rough old night"; "her daughter's hand"; "the stormy darkness"*)
  - five descriptive verbs ending in *-ed* (e.g. *"snatched", "slammed", "slipped", "loosed", "stepped", "explained", "raised", "spurred", "swallowed"*).

- Discuss the fact that using language so precisely allows the author to spend less time on long descriptions, so he only describes what the reader needs to know and understand.
- Ask the children to look again at the final paragraph. Can they find one place where:
  - something is compared to something else (*"as light as thistledown"*)
  - something is described as something else (*"the full white moon of her face"*).
    - Talk about the impact of this kind of descriptive language on the reader's understanding of the story. (If your class are interested, introduce the words *simile* (comparing something to something else, e.g. *"as light as thistledown"*) and *metaphor* (saying something is something else, e.g. *"the full white moon of her face"*.)
- Ask children to find their storm thesaurus from Stage 1 (above). Challenge them to add five new words or phrases to it from this text.

Looking at paragraphs

- *Think, pair, share:* Why do writers use paragraphs? (E.g. *To organise and link ideas clearly for the reader; to introduce new sections of a story; to show when a new speaker is talking.*)
  - Remind children of common reasons for beginning new paragraphs:
  - (a) New speaker in dialogue
  - (b) New/change of event or action
  - (c) New/change of place
  - (d) New/change of time
  - (e) New/change of character.
  - Together discuss why the author began each new paragraph for the first few paragraphs.
  - In pairs, ask children to write a letter from the list above beside each paragraph of the enlarged copy of the story, indicating why the author began a new paragraph, e.g.
    - Paragraph 1: introduction
    - Paragraph 2: new action
    - Paragraph 3: new speaker
    - Paragraph 4: change of characters
    - Paragraph 5: new action
    - Paragraph 6: new action
    - Paragraph 7: new speaker
    - Paragraph 8: new speaker, etc.

    Clarify that paragraphs are useful for making a text look less scary to read, but they also help the reader to understand the sequence of events and ideas.

Looking at punctuation

- In pairs, ask children to highlight all the apostrophes they can find. Then ask them to list the words containing apostrophes in two sets:
  - apostrophes showing ownership: (*Carters', mother's, Annie's, daughter's*)
  - apostrophe showing missing letters: (*can't, don't, there's, that's, there's*).
    - Clarify any misconceptions.
    - Check that all children are able to expand the contracted forms and can find the hidden verbs in *there is* and *that is*.
- Ask children to highlight six exclamation marks.
  - Discuss why the author used this punctuation instead of full stops. Which emotion is he trying to convey?

Stage 4: Planning to write: Writing a story with a strong setting

Activities:

- Ask children to read the text aloud to a response partner while thinking how paragraphs and punctuation help the reader to read with fluency and expression.

Thinking about story ideas

- Tell children they're going to plan their own story about a rescue during a storm. Together discuss and agree some of the ideas they could use for a setting (e.g. *city, countryside, garden, mountain, seaside, at sea, Arctic*) and a person, pet, creature or thing that could be rescued.

  - In groups, ask children to divide a large sheet of paper into four equal spaces and label each space with a different place such as the examples given above.

  - Under each place, they should discuss, agree and list:

    - a person, pet, creature, toy or thing that is to be rescued

    - why the person/creature/thing needs to be rescued

    - how the storm might make the rescue difficult.

- Children should:

  - talk through each of the story ideas, all contributing suggestions to improve the development of the idea

  - in pairs, choose one of the ideas to retell to each other.

Planning in pairs

- Distribute the writing framework.
- Select an idea from those explored earlier and model using the writing framework to record and develop it.

  - In the first box, children should briefly list key elements from their story idea.

  - Explain that the numbered boxes are for them to write or draw a brief summary for each phase of the story.

- Model improving on your plan by recording some words about the storm, including some ideas for imagery.
- Working in pairs, the children should add as much detail as is useful to their plans. Suggest that they jot down adverbs or words from their storm thesaurus for each section of their story.
- Give each child the opportunity to 'talk like a writer' to a different response partner to say how they think the story will develop and to receive peer feedback.
- Ask the children what they think a story about a successful rescue should include. Compare to the success criteria (online at My Rising Stars) and amend if necessary.
- Clarify the success criteria.

Resources needed:

Shared copy of the text (PDF/IWB/visualiser)

The success criteria

Each group needs:

- large paper.

Each child needs:

- the copy of the text they have previously highlighted and annotated
- the 'storm' thesaurus from Stage 1
- marker pens/coloured pencils
- the writing framework from page 50 (some children may benefit from this being enlarged to A3).

Stage 5: Writing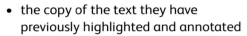

Activities:

- Remind children that they are going to write their own story about a rescue during a storm.
- Model using your plan to write part of the story. Ensure you include: more than one paragraph, descriptions of the setting and the weather (including a comparative noun phrase with a strong image, e.g. *the storm was like a tantrum*), descriptive verbs, layered storm vocabulary as well as exclamations to show the feelings of a character.
- Give children a few minutes to 'talk like a writer' and tell another response partner the story as they plan to write it. If it helps, ask them to use a polite 'writer's voice'. Remind them to use their plan and not to invent another story as they go along.
- Let response partners give some brief feedback before children swap roles.
- Tell children your expectations about how much space each part of the story will take up on the page, e.g.
  - Introduction: 2–3 lines
  - Problem: 4–5 lines
  - Action: 4–5 lines
  - Outcome: 3–4 lines
  - Ending: 2–3 lines.

  (Amend these line numbers for your class and the amount of time they have to write.)
- Remind children they can compose and rehearse sentences inside their head or in a low whisper before they begin to write them.
- Read aloud the success criteria (online at My Rising Stars).
- Let the children write. Break up the process. Talk about the focus for each paragraph and quickly model a sentence or idea that the children could try out in their writing.
- Five minutes before the end of the stage, ask all children to stop writing and read their story aloud to themselves. If they find errors, missing words words they can improve, they should use this opportunity to make changes.

Resources needed:

Each child needs:

- the copy of the text they have previously highlighted and annotated
- their 'storm' thesaurus
- the completed writing framework.

Stage 6: Improving, editing, reviewing and sharing the writing

Activities:

- Revisit together the success criteria (online at My Rising Stars).
- Model the process below using your work as an example. The children can give you feedback on each step of the process. After you model a step, the children should have a go with their partner at editing their own work.
- Ask children to reread their texts three times with their response partner:
  - First read through: Children read their partner's text out loud to them. The child who wrote the text listens to check that their writing makes sense, listens out for obvious errors and checks the text follows their plan. Children then swap roles.
  - Second read through: Children read their partner's text and highlight the success criteria they have met. They suggest three places where their partner could improve their work (to achieve or further improve on the success criteria).
  - Third read through: Children proofread their partner's text together with them. They check for errors in punctuation and spelling and correct these as necessary. You should give input at this stage if needed.

Resources needed:

Each child needs:

- the success criteria
- their writing/completed writing framework
- different coloured highlighters/pens/pencils.

Lessons from writing

- Prior to the session, identify errors that were commonly made. Write sample sentences that need to be corrected and ask the children to help you to fix them. These could include:

  - overuse of storm language for no particular purpose, e.g. *Thunder rumbled and rolled like a storm at sea and the wind howled and shrieked like an angry monster as Johanne got closer to the cave. He was as wet as if he had been swimming in his clothes and as frightened as someone in a graveyard at midnight.*

    - Help children to identify the phrases that help the reader to visualise the scene and to edit other information.

  - inconsistent tense and person, e.g. *Tam was bent almost double as he walked into the wind. I'm not doing this again I said. I turn round and let the wind blow me back downhill. Then Tam went home again.*

    - Ask children to correct the mistakes.
    - Discuss how difficult it is to keep track of events in a story when the writing is confused like this.

Improving the writing

- **After the stories have been marked:** give the children time to read through your comments, to look at the success criteria and to implement any changes suggested. This should not involve the children rewriting the entire story – just those parts that you would like them to revisit to practise/improve their writing.

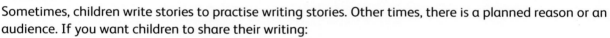

Share

Sometimes, children write stories to practise writing stories. Other times, there is a planned reason or an audience. If you want children to share their writing:

- they can copy it out in presentation handwriting; however, this should be regarded simply as a handwriting activity not as another opportunity to improve the text – the rewritten text should be used for a specific audience or display

- create a stormy display featuring the writing frameworks and artwork as well as well-presented stories

- let children rehearse and make audio recordings of their stories with dramatic reading and sound effects.

Unit 4: Writing a story with a strong setting

Name: Class: Date:

In the boxes below, draw or write your ideas for a story about a rescue in a storm.

Where is the story set? Who or what is rescued? How does the storm make it difficult? **1 Introduction**	**2 Problem**
3 Action	**4 Outcome**
	5 Ending

Unit 4: Moderating writing: Writing a story with a strong setting

Name: Date:

	Contents	Text structure and organisation	Sentence structure	Vocabulary and descriptions	Punctuation	Spelling and handwriting
Working at greater depth within the expected standard	Characters and settings are consistent and convincing.	Paragraphs introduce a change of speaker, time, place or action.	The story is consistently written in the past tense, except in dialogue.	More sophisticated vocabulary is used to create atmosphere.	Inverted commas and other punctuation are used in dialogue.	Spelling changes needed to add vowel suffixes are often accurate.
	At least one additional detail is included to help the reader to engage with the text.	The story has a satisfying shape leading to an exciting action, outcome and ending.	Appropriate choice of pronouns avoids repetition.	Noun phrases may be extended with prepositional phrases.	Apostrophes are only used in appropriate contexts.	In handwriting, most letters are appropriately joined or word-processing speed is developing and does not impede thought processes.
Working at the expected standard	A story about a rescue in a storm is written.	Paragraphs are used to distinguish different sections in the story.	Some paragraphs begin with an adverb to show a change of time or place.	Some thoughtful choices of technical vocabulary (linked to storms) are included.	Some paragraphs begin with an adverb to show a change of time or place.	A range of prefixes is used to form nouns.
			The text includes at least two different types of sentence.		The text includes at least two different types of sentence.	Taught spellings from the Year 3/4 word list are correct.
	Some attempt is made to develop character and setting.	The story leads towards a single interesting event.	Conjunction, adverbs and prepositions are used to show when, where and why events occur.	Descriptive verbs make the action fast paced.	End of sentence punctuation (.?!) is generally accurate.	Some letters are joined using diagonal or horizontal strokes.
					Commas are used to separate items in lists.	Letters and spaces are in proportion to each other.
Working towards the expected standard	The story follows the plan.	Ideas are grouped and sequenced appropriately.	At least three different conjunctions are used correctly.	Some expanded noun phrases are used to describe and specify.	End of sentence punctuation (.?!) is often accurate.	Spelling errors are phonetically decodable.
	The story includes a storm.		Most of the story is in the past tense.	Some storm-related vocabulary is used.	Apostrophes are used for contractions (missing letters).	Spaces between letters and words allow for good legibility.

Real Live Dragons!

Did you know that many different kinds of creatures are called dragons? They may not be as exciting as some of the dragons you read about in stories, but they are real, live dragons.

Komodo dragon

The Komodo dragon is the world's biggest lizard. They can't breathe fire, but they do inject venom into their prey. The venom speeds up blood loss. Even if a pig, deer or buffalo escapes the Komodo's attack, it quickly weakens and dies so the dragon can eat in its own good time.

Lives in: Indonesia

Eats: meat including pig, deer, buffalo

Size: up to 300 cm long

Dragonsnake

The dragonsnake is called 'dragon' because it has three ridges of knobbly scales that run down its body. Dragonsnakes mostly bask in the sun during the hottest parts of the day and hunt for frogs at night.

Lives in: Burma, Thailand and Indonesia

Eats: mostly frogs

Size: up to 100 cm long

Dragon millipede

This bright pink minibeast is found throughout Asia. It has spikes around the tops of its legs for protection. Its bright colour warns predators that the millipede is dangerous and it can spray a strong venom when it is under attack.

Lives in: Asia

Eats: insects

Size: 3 cm long

Flying dragon

Flying dragons have special flaps of skin over their ribs so they can glide from tree to tree. Some can glide as far as 60 m. They live in rainforests.

Lives in: South East Asia

Eats: insects

Size: 22 cm long

Bearded dragon

This lizard has a fringed ruff around its throat which it can puff out to make a ring of spiked scales around its neck. This 'beard' turns black when the dragon is angry. Some bearded dragons can change colour when they bask in the sun.

Lives in: Australia

Eats: fruit, vegetables, insects

Size: up to 60 cm long

Name: Class: Date:

1. Tick **three** things the text says are true about Komodo dragons.

    They breathe fire.   ☐

    They inject a venom into their prey.   ☐

    They eat crocodiles.   ☐

    They are lizards.   ☐

    They live in Indonesia.   ☐

2. Dragonsnakes "*mostly* bask *in the sun during the hottest part of the day*".
    In this sentence, tick **one** word that *bask* is closest to in meaning.

    bake   ☐   exercise   ☐

    hunt   ☐   relax   ☐

3. What colour are dragon millipedes?

    _____

4. How do flying dragons fly?

    _____

5. (a) What makes an angry bearded dragon look scary?

        _____

    (b) Should you be frightened of a bearded dragon?   Yes ☐   No ☐

        Explain your answer.

        _____

6. Number these dragons 1–5 in order of size (largest to smallest). One has been done for you:

    Komodo dragon   [1]

    Dragonsnake   [   ]

    Dragon millipede   [   ]

    Flying dragon   [   ]

    Bearded dragon   [   ]

Unit 5 Writing a report/information text

In this unit children will:

- read a report/information text
- use headings and paragraphs to understand the structure and organisation of the text
- identify coordinating and subordinating conjunctions, and discuss their function and impact
- look at how noun phrases are expanded with accurate, technical vocabulary
- plan, draft, edit and improve an information/report text.

Stage 1: Responding to the text

Activities:

- Establish prior knowledge.
- *Think, pair, share:* Ask pairs of children to list what they know about dragons. Their list could include:
  - stories or films with dragons
  - myths with dragons
  - video games with dragons
  - komodo dragons or other lizards.
    - Tactfully discuss the differences between 'real dragons' and dragons in stories, bearing in mind some children may not be clear about the distinction.
- What do children know about information/report texts that tell about how things are now? List expectations of a text called 'Real Live Dragons!', e.g.
  - non-fiction text – an information text, not a story
  - it will tell the reader about different kinds of dragons
  - it may have headings and fact boxes.
- Show the children the text: without reading it, what are the layout clues that it's non-fiction? (E.g. *headings, fact boxes, photographs with each section.*)
- Before reading the text ensure the children understand the meaning of the more unusual words and phrases: *"lizard", "venom", "bask", "glide", "predator", "fringed ruff"* and *"protection"*. Help the children remember the meanings of these words by putting them in contextualising sentences, e.g. *I love to lie out in the hot sun, just basking in the heat.*
- Read and talk about the text.
  - Were the expectations of the features of non-fiction texts accurate?
  - Can they add anything else to their list? (E.g. *present tense.*)
  - What did the children find out from this text that they didn't know before?
- Ask the children to answer the reading comprehension questions to ensure close reading of the text and good understanding.
- Together, share answers to the questions and discuss the strategies children used to answer them. Break down how to answer question 5. Help children to make their opinion based on evidence from the text.

Resources needed:

Shared copy of the text (PDF/IWB/visualiser)

Each child needs:

- a copy of the text
- a copy of the comprehension questions.

Stage 2: Analysing the text structure and organisation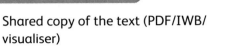

Activities:

- Ask children to read the text aloud to a response partner to revisit the text, develop fluency, ensure appropriate pronunciation of all words and to practise reading with good intonation and expression.
- Ask children to underline any new words or phrases. Take feedback and explain what these mean in context.

Resources needed:

Shared copy of the text (PDF/IWB/visualiser)

Each pair needs:

- a spare copy of the text and scissors

Each child needs:

- a copy of the text
- coloured highlighters/pencils (each child/pair needs the same three colours).

Analysing paragraphs

- Talk first about the headings:
  - What do they tell us? (E.g. *They tell you which creature the text is going to be about.*)
  - How do they make the text easier to read? (E.g. *By telling the reader what each paragraph is about.*)
  - Why are they where they are in the text? (E.g. *They introduce new topics.*)
- Model reading the first paragraph aloud and work with the children to identify the most interesting piece of information to underline (e.g. *many different kinds of creatures are called dragons*). Discuss why you chose this piece of information.
- Ask children to work in pairs:
  - Child 1 reads the next paragraph aloud. Child 2 has to identify the most interesting piece of information to underline (e.g. *"world's biggest lizards"*).
  - Children should continue until the end of the text, swapping roles each time.
  - Children should then revisit the 'best fact' they found in each paragraph.
- Let each pair compare their 'best fact' with another pair. Are they broadly the same? If there are discrepancies, suggest the pairs seek advice from a third pair.
- Discuss as a class what the most interesting piece of information is in each paragraph.
  - Do the children largely agree?
  - Is the best fact often found in the first sentence or are they distributed around the paragraph?

Discussing organisation

- *Think pair, share:* Ask children in their pairs to:
  - cut the text up, paragraph by paragraph, keeping headings and text boxes with the paragraph
    - Explore different ways of rearranging the text.
    - Does it matter which order the reader reads each of the paragraphs? (*Yes – the first paragraph must be read first because it introduces the rest of the paragraphs. It doesn't matter in which order the dragons are read about.*)
  - discuss how the organisation of paragraphs is different in this report/information text from a story. (E.g. *In stories, paragraph order matters because they usually describe a sequence of events. In a report/information text like this, there is no need for a particular order. We can call these texts non-chronological. 'Chronological' means in time or in sequence. The paragraphs in this text do not have to be read in any sequence.*)

Stage 3: Analysing the text purpose and language

Activities:

Discussing text purpose

- Ask groups of children to reread the text and discuss its purpose. Give them a choice between:
    - to tell a story
    - to explain how or why something happens
    - to talk about an experience someone had
    - to say what something is like.
- Ask groups to think about *how* they know the purpose of the text. Ask them to consider the meaning/contents of the text (e.g. *it tells us what the dragons are like and what they can do*).
- Ask them to discuss the purpose of layout features including:
    - headings
    - paragraphs
    - introduction
    - text boxes.

Discussing language

- Discuss why the opening sentence is a question. (*It tells you what the text will be about/it makes the reader want to know the answer.*)
- *Think, pair, share:* Is this text written in the past or present tense? (*Present.*)
    - How do you know? (*Look at the verbs, e.g. "are", "do", "can" and verb endings, e.g. "speeds", "escapes", "weakens".*)
    - Why is it in the present tense? (*Because it describes what something is like now.*)
- Can children tell you what conjunctions do in a text? (*Link words, phrases or clauses.*)
- Identify the different functions of conjunctions, e.g.
    - coordinating conjunctions like *and, but, or, so* can link words and phrases (e.g. *"pig, deer <u>or</u> buffalo"*)
    - coordinating conjunctions also link two clauses (e.g. *"they can't breathe fire <u>but</u> they do inject venom"*).
        - Sometimes words like '*they*' are not repeated (e.g. *"They mostly bask in the sun during the hottest parts of the day <u>and</u> hunt for frogs at night"*) but you can easily work out what they should be.
    - subordinating conjunctions (e.g. *because, although, that, when, before, after, while*) link a main clause and a subordinate clause; the subordinate clause adds new information which tells us more about the main clause (e.g. *"The dragonsnake is called 'dragon' <u>because</u> it has three ridges of knobbly scales that run down its body; Some bearded dragons can change colour <u>when</u> they bask in the sun"*).
- Some sentences have both coordinating and subordinating conjunctions (e.g. *"Its bright colour warns predators <u>that</u> the millipede is dangerous* **and** *it can spray a strong venom <u>when</u> it is under attack.*").
- Tell children that most clauses can have only one verb, so if there is more than one verb in a sentence they should look for a connective.
- Discuss why this text has more conjunctions (which link ideas and often explain why things happen) than adverbs or prepositions which tell as where and when they happen (e.g. *we may not need to know* where and when *things happen in a non-chronological, non-fiction text like this one*).

Discussing vocabulary

- In pairs, ask children to highlight unusual dragon-related vocabulary.
  - Ask more confident children to suggest definitions for each word. Do they need to look outside the text or does the text contain enough information?
  - Discuss reasons why the writer used this more challenging vocabulary when writing this text (e.g. *to show it is non-fiction; there aren't any other accurate words; these words describe something particular*).
  - Clarify that writers of non-fiction often need to use particular words which are accurate.
  - Give pairs of children dragon words from the text and ask them to write a definition of their word. Collect all the definitions to make an alphabetically ordered glossary.
- Allocate paragraphs to pairs of children and ask them to circle all noun phrases which include adjectives (e.g. "*real, live dragons*"; "*many different kinds*"; "*the world's biggest lizards*"; "*its own good time*"; "*three ridges*"; "*knobbly scales*"; "*the hottest parts*"; "*bright pink minibeast*"; "*its bright colour*"; "*a strong venom*"; "*a fringed ruff*").
  - Children may also identify prepositional phrases used to modify noun phrases (e.g. "*three ridges of knobbly scales*"; "*the hottest parts of the day*"; "*special flaps of skin over their ribs*"; "*a fringed ruff around their throats*"; "*a ring of spiked scales*"). Explain that this is a more advanced way of giving more information about the noun.
- Discuss the function of expanded noun phrases in the text (e.g. *improves the reader's ability to understand what they are reading about*).

Stage 4: Planning to write: Writing a report/information text 🖊

Activities:

- Prior to the session, decide what you'd like the children to write an information report about. The given example is 'Pets', but you can easily amend it to fit in with a curriculum topic for which children have done some research.
- Tell the children they are going to be writing an information report about (e.g. 'Pets').
- In groups ask children to:
  - list 5–10 familiar pets
  - orally, share information about the pets; this could include:
    - the kind of creatures they are and other related creatures
    - why people have them as pets
    - what they look like
    - any illnesses they get
    - how they need to be looked after
    - what they eat
    - how big they are.
- Distribute the writing framework.
  - Choose a pet and model completing the plan.
  - Ask children to work in pairs to agree which of the pets they want to write about and which pet facts they choose to use. They should record these in note form on the writing framework. (If they wish to record more than three facts they can add more on the reverse of the sheet.)
  - Ask children to discuss, rehearse and record an opening question and think about what they would write in the introduction. They can record notes on the reverse of the sheet.

Resources needed:

Shared copy of the text (PDF/IWB/visualiser)

The success criteria

Groups of children need:

- a flipchart/large paper and marker pens
- access to the internet or relevant non-fiction books for research

Each child needs:

- the copy of the text they have previously highlighted and annotated
- the writing framework from page 61 (some children may benefit from this being enlarged to A3).

- Let children talk through their plan with a different response partner who can indicate whether the text makes sense.
- Give each child the opportunity to 'talk like a writer' to a different response partner to rehearse the structure and language of their text and to receive peer feedback.
- Ask the children to decide what a successful information text should include. Compare this to the success criteria (online at My Rising Stars) and amend if necessary.
- Clarify the success criteria.

Stage 5: Writing

Activities:

- Remind children that they are going to write an information report about pets (or whatever topic you chose).
- Model using your plan to write the introductory paragraph. Ensure you include the features that you have explored: question to open the paragraph, third person, present tense, sentences with more than one clause and expanded noun phrases.
- Give children a few minutes to 'talk like a writer' and orally rehearse the text as they plan to write it. If it helps, ask them to use a polite 'writer's voice'. Remind them to use their plan.
- Let response partners give some brief feedback before children swap roles.
- Tell children your expectations about how much space each part of the story will take up on the page, e.g.
  - Introduction: 2–3 lines
  - Each pet: 4–5 lines.
  (Amend these line numbers for your class and the amount of time they have to write.)
- Remind children they can compose and rehearse sentences inside their head or in a low whisper before they begin to write them.
- Read aloud the success criteria (online at My Rising Stars).
- Let the children write. Break up the process. Talk about the focus for each paragraph and quickly model a sentence or idea that the children could try out in their writing.
- Five minutes before the end of the stage, ask all children to stop writing and read their story aloud to themselves. If they find errors, or missing words or words they can improve, they should use this opportunity to make changes.

Resources needed:

The success criteria

Each child needs:

- the copy of the text they have previously highlighted and annotated
- the completed writing framework
- a PC/laptop/tablet if the children are word-processing.

Stage 6: Improving, editing, reviewing and sharing the writing

Activities:

- Revisit together the success criteria (online at My Rising Stars).
- Model the process below using your work as an example. The children can give you feedback on each step of the process. After you model a step the children should have a go with their partner at editing their own work.

Resources needed:

Each child needs:

- the success criteria
- their writing/completed writing framework
- different coloured highlighters/pens.

- Ask children to reread their texts three times with their response partner:
  - First read through: Children read their partner's text out loud to them. The child who wrote the text listens to check that their writing makes sense, listens out for obvious errors and checks the text follows their plan. Children then swap roles.
  - Second read through: Children read their partner's text and highlight the success criteria they have met. They suggest three places where their partner could improve their work (to achieve or further improve on the success criteria).
  - Third read through: Children proofread their partner's text together with them. They check for errors in punctuation and spelling and correct these as necessary. You should give input at this stage if needed.

Lessons from writing

- Prior to the session, identify errors that were commonly made. Write sample sentences that need to be corrected and ask the children to help you to fix them. These could include:
  - inconsistent use of tense, e.g. *Cats are easy to look after. You have to feed them every day. They also needed water. Cats like to go outside so they could go to the toilet in the garden but some cats used a litter tray inside.*
    - Ask children to identify the errors and clarify that most information report texts are written in the present tense.
  - inconsistent use of third person, e.g. *Labradors are medium sized dogs. We take our Labrador for walks. She loves running on the beach. Labradors have to have walks every day so they don't get fat.*
    - Ask children to identify the errors and clarify that most information report texts are written using words/ pronouns like *it, they* not *I, we*.

Improving the writing

- **After the texts have been marked:** give the children time to read through your comments, to look at the success criteria and to implement any changes suggested. This should not involve the children rewriting the entire text – just those parts that you would like them to revisit to practise/improve their writing.

> ### Share
>
> Sometimes, children write text to practise writing text. Other times, there is a planned reason or an audience. If you want children to share their writing:
>
> - they can collaborate with a response partner to improve the text for publication; this could involve importing and labelling images of the pets – the combined pages could become an e-book or a printed book for a younger class
> - let children collect and collate images and video of their chosen pets and use their text as an audio track to an online presentation.

Name: Class: Date:

1: _____

Fact 1	Fact 2	Fact 3	Fact file

2: _____

Fact 1	Fact 2	Fact 3	Fact file

3: _____

Fact 1	Fact 2	Fact 3	Fact file Eats: Size:

Make notes of what you will include in your introduction and include an opening question.

Unit 5: Moderating writing: Writing a report/information text

Name: Date:

Standard	Contents	Text structure and organisation	Sentence structure	Vocabulary and descriptions	Punctuation	Spelling and handwriting
Working **at greater depth** within the expected standard	Fact files follow the example from the model text and add new information.	Paragraphs are generally used to group related ideas.	Appropriate choice of pronouns is used to avoid repetition.	More sophisticated vocabulary is used.	Apostrophes are use accurately.	Spelling changes needed to add vowel suffixes are often accurate.
		The text is logically organised.	Standard English verb inflections are used (e.g. I was, we were, etc.).	Noun phrases may be expanded with prepositional phrases.		In handwriting, most letters are appropriately joined or word-processing speed is developing and does not impede thought processes.
Working **at** the expected standard	An information/report text about pets is written.	Paragraphs are often used to group related ideas.	Each paragraph is about a different topic.	Some thoughtful choices of topic-related vocabulary (linked to pets) is included.	Question marks are used at the end of a question.	A range of prefixes and suffixes is used.
		A short introduction gives an overview of the topic.	The text includes at least two different types of sentence.		Most sentences are punctuated with a full stop.	Taught spellings from the Year 3/4 word list are correct.
			Coordinating conjunctions (e.g. and, or, but) are used to link ideas.	Expanded noun phrases are used to describe and specify.	Commas may be used to separate items in lists.	Some letters are joined using diagonal or horizontal strokes.
			Subordinating conjunctions (e.g. because, when, until) are used to add information.			Letters and spaces are in proportion to each other.
Working **towards** the expected standard	The text follows the plan.	Ideas are grouped appropriately.	At least two different conjunctions are used correctly.	Some relevant vocabulary is used.	End of sentence punctuation (.?!) is often accurate.	Spelling errors are phonetically decodable.
			Most of the text is in the present tense.	A few noun phrases are expanded with adjectives.	Apostrophes are used for contractions (missing letters).	Spaces between letters and words allow for good legibility.

How Do Your Senses Work?

Your body has lots of ways of finding out about the world around you. It uses things called senses. You have five main senses. You can touch with your skin, see with your eyes, hear with your ears, taste with your tongue and smell with your nose. You use one or more of your senses to discover everything you know about the world around you.

Your eyes, ears, skin, nose and tongue send messages to your brain. The messages travel along pathways called nerves. Your brain gets the message and decides what to do.

How does touch work?

Your skin can feel things that it touches so you know more about what you are touching. Your body can tell whether something is hot or cold, soft or hard, tickly or scratchy, heavy or light or many other feelings and sensations.

Your skin can feel because it has lots of tiny touch receptors. These are tiny cells that respond when you touch something. They feel different things and can then send messages to your brain.

Some parts of your body are better at feeling than others because they have lots of touch receptors in them. These parts of your body, like your mouth and lips, the palms of your hands and the soles of your feet, can feel very well.

What happens inside the body when we touch something?

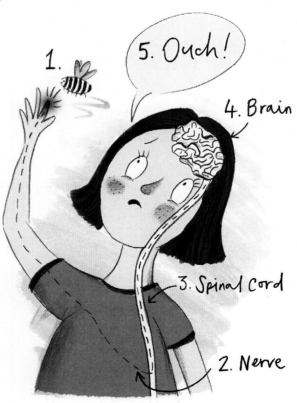

1. The bee stings the girl's hand.

2. The touch receptors in her skin send messages along the nerves in her arm to her spine. Inside her spine is her spinal cord.

3. The messages zoom up her spinal cord to her brain.

4. Her brain tells her hand that she has been hurt.

5. Messages rush from her brain back down different nerves in her arm telling her to pull her hand away. At the same time, messages rush to her mouth so she says "ouch".

Unit 6: How Do Your Senses Work?

Name: Class: Date:

1. Draw lines to match the sense and the way we receive it. Write an answer in the empty box.

    | sight | | ears |
    | smell | | tongue |
    | touch | | eyes |
    | hearing | | nose |
    | taste | | |

2. What do we call the pathways along which messages pass to your brain?

    _____

3. What are *"touch receptors"*? Tick **one**.

    cells at the top of the skin   ☐

    cells that can sense what you touch   ☐

    the youngest cells in the skin   ☐

    cells that use all five senses   ☐

4. Why do you think you need more touch receptors in the skin on your hand than in the skin on your back?

    _____

5. Number the events to show the order in which they happen. The first one has been done for you.

    Messages reach the brain.   ☐

    Touch receptors send message along the nerve.   ☐

    Messages go up the spinal cord.   ☐

    Something touches the skin.   [1]

6. Why do you think the writer has used a diagram with labels beside the final piece of text?
    Tick **one**.

    It makes the page look pretty.   ☐

    So the reader knows what hurt the girl.   ☐

    To show you what the girl said when she was hurt.   ☐

    To help the reader understand the text.   ☐

Unit 6 Writing an explanatory text

In this unit children will:

- read an explanatory text
- consider the function and structure of paragraphs in organising information, including identifying topic sentences
- recognise second and third person writing
- look for technical, subject-specific vocabulary
- plan, draft, edit and improve an explanatory text.

Stage 1: Responding to the text

Activities:

- Establish prior knowledge. What do children know about their senses?
  - Start a class mind map about senses.
    - Which senses can children think of? (*Sight, hearing, touch, taste, smell.*)
    - Create branches on your mind map for different senses. Take a few ideas from the children to begin to populate them (e.g. *list the organ that receives the information; what the sense is useful for; what kinds of sensation it can sense; attractive and disagreeable sensations; vocabulary linked to that sense*).
  - Ask the children to work in pairs to think of three more pieces of information they could add for each sense. Ask them to write each idea on a separate sticky note and attach them to your mind map.
  - Group and summarise the children's ideas by adding to your class mind map.
- Before reading the text, ensure the children understand the meaning of the more unusual words and phrases: "*sensations*", "*receptors*", "*respond*", "*pathways (called nerves)*", *spine*" and "*spinal cord*".
- Help the children remember the meanings of these words by putting them in contextualising sentences, e.g. *I can feel the cold as the water falls on my hand: it is a shivery sensation.*
- Read and talk about the text.
  - Ask the children to think about all the ways in which their brain receives information about the world around them. Can they think of any others? (E.g. *Balance and proprioception – knowing where the body is in space.*)
  - Clarify that *all* information about the world is received via one or more of these senses.
- Let children answer the reading comprehension questions to ensure close reading of the text and good understanding.
- Together, share answers to the questions and discuss the strategies children used to answer them. Help children to work out the answer to question 5, sequencing the events.

Resources needed:

Shared copy of the text (PDF/IWB/visualiser)

- whiteboard or large paper

Each child needs:

- sticky notes
- a copy of the text
- a copy of the comprehension questions.

Stage 2: Analysing the text structure and organisation

Activities:

- Ask children to read the text aloud to a response partner to revisit the text, develop fluency, ensure appropriate pronunciation of all words and to practise reading with good intonation and expression.
- Ask children to underline any words or phrases. Take feedback and explain what these mean in context.

Resources needed:

Shared copy of the text (PDF/IWB/visualiser)

Each child needs:

- a copy of the text
- different coloured highlighters/pencils (each child/pair needs the same three colours).

Analysing paragraphs

- Talk first about the headings.
  - Why has the writer written them as questions?
  - Why are they where they are in the text?
  - Could they move and be between different paragraphs, or even inside paragraphs? Why not?
- Model reading the first paragraph aloud and work with the children to identify the most important piece of information to underline (e.g. *"You use one or more of your senses to discover everything you know about the world"*). Discuss why you chose that piece of information.
- Ask children to work in pairs:
  - Child 1 reads the next paragraph aloud. Child 2 has to identify the most important piece of information to underline. Children should write down what they think each paragraph is about.
  - Children should continue until the end of the text, swapping roles each time.

  Tell them to stop when they reach the last section with the numbered list.

- Let each pair compare their important information with another pair. Are they broadly the same? If any of the paragraphs has been given a different focus, suggest the pairs seek advice from a third pair.
- Discuss as a class what each paragraph is about.
- Read the topic sentences (the first sentence in each paragraph) aloud to the children. Are these very different from the key information sentences the children wrote? Explain that in non-fiction texts, the opening sentence of a paragraph – called the topic sentence – usually tells you what the paragraph is about.
- Ask children to underline the topic sentences for each paragraph.

Discussing organisation

- Give children three section titles and allocate a colour to each one:
  - general introduction (e.g. *orange*)
  - subject information (e.g. *green*)
  - more detailed subject information (e.g. *yellow*).
    - Model reading the first paragraph and deciding what kind of information it gives (*general introduction*).
    - Ask children to work in pairs and use the colours as suggested to circle different parts of the text according to the kind of information it gives.
- Discuss their decisions. The recommendation is:
  - Section 1: paragraphs 1 and 2 are a general introduction to the senses
  - Section 2: paragraphs 3, 4, and 5 give some subject information about touch
  - Section 3: the list and diagram give more detailed information about how touch works.

  If children have different answers, discuss their ideas.

- Talk about *why* the writer used this sequence of ideas, i.e. from the bigger picture, to the smaller. Would the text make more or less sense if the sections were rearranged?

- Clarify that many non-fiction texts follow the same pattern: they start with a big picture, then increasingly narrow the focus. Discuss how that is different from the organisation of events in a story.
- If children were going to add a new part to this text which discussed a different sense, e.g. hearing, would they need to write all three sections again? Clarify that the opening paragraphs, which give a general introduction, would still be appropriate so they would only need to write sections two and three.

Stage 3: Analysing the text purpose and language

Activities:

Discussing text purpose

- Ask groups of children to reread the text and discuss the main purpose of each of the sections. Give them a choice between:
  - to tell a story
  - to explain how or why something happens (this is the main purpose)
  - to talk about an experience someone had
  - to say what something is like.
- Ask children how they would know the difference between:
  - a report text telling you what something is like
  - an explanatory text telling you how something happens (for explanations, look for the type of information given as well as the use of subordinating conjunctions such as *because, so, if, that, when*).
- Model reading the first paragraph in each section with the children. Talk first about the information and whether it tells you what something is or how something happens. Then look for conjunctions. Agree that the opening paragraph is a report, whereas paragraph three is an explanation.
- Ask children to annotate their texts, so they write the purpose beside each section. Warn the children that some of the sections have similar purposes, but that they don't all have the same purpose.
- Let each group feed back to the class, explaining the decisions they made.
- The recommendation is:
  - Section 1: to say what something is (*report text*). This section tells you what senses are.
  - Section 2: to say how something works (*explanatory text*). This section tells you how you feel things.
  - Section 3: to say how or why something happens (*explanatory text*). This section explains the process by which the brain learns about how something feels.
- Ask children to suggest an overall purpose for the text and to justify their suggestions. Since the structure of the text is to give information about what something is *in order to* explain how it works, the overall purpose would generally be agreed to be explanatory.

Second and third person

- Talk about the fact that:
  - some texts are written from the writer's point of view and use words such as (pronouns) *I, me, mine* and (possessive determiner) *my*
  - some texts talk directly to the reader and use words such as (pronouns) *you, yours* and (possessive determiner) *your*
  - some texts talk about something or someone and use words such as (pronouns) *it, she, they* and (possessive determiner) *her, its, their*.

Resources needed:

Shared copy of the text (PDF/IWB/visualiser)

Each child needs:

- the copy of the text
- different coloured highlighters/pens/pencils.

- Ask children to scan the text for these words and to circle those they find.
  - Discuss why the writer chose to use lots of second person words in the first two sections (e.g. *to make the reader feel involved*).
  - Why might the writer have changed to third person words in the final section (e.g. *because the picture shows a girl and boys may object; the writer wants to show that this process is true of all people*).

Analysing vocabulary

- Ask children to highlight technical terms about the body that they are introduced to in the text (e.g. *"sense"*, *"nerve"*, *"touch receptor"*, etc.).
- Ask pairs of children to write glossary definitions for each. Do they need to look outside the text or does the text contain enough information?
- Discuss why the writer gives information explaining what each of the technical words mean.
- Discuss reasons why the writer used technical vocabulary when writing this text.

Stage 4: Planning to write: Writing an explanatory text

Activities:

- Tell the children that they are going to continue the text, writing about a different sense.
- Together, revisit the senses mind map that you made at Stage 1.
- Add as much new information as you can about touch, using the information from the text.
- Let groups choose a different sense. Ask them to research the new sense in order to add more information to the relevant section of your mind map. Remind them that they need to find out *how* the body understands the sensation as well as what kind of things we can do with the sense. (Children who struggle with research, or all children if you want to save time, could use the notes at the foot of the writing framework as the basis for writing about hearing.)
- Give pairs of children large sheets of paper. Ask them to work together to plan and draft some text they can use and to draft a diagram of that sense being understood.
- Introduce the writing framework. Read the information in the panels to the left aloud to the children so that they know what kind of information they will need to make notes about in each section.
- Model using the writing framework to make notes about hearing using information from the foot of the sheet together with information from your mind map.
- Ask the children to decide what a successful explanatory text should include. Compare this to the success criteria (online at My Rising Stars) and amend if necessary.
- Clarify the success criteria.

Resources needed:

Shared copy of the text (PDF/IWB/visualiser)

The success criteria

Pairs of children need:

- a flipchart/large paper and marker pens
- access to the internet or relevant non-fiction books for research

Each child needs:

- the copy of the text they have previously highlighted and annotated
- the mind map from Stage 1
- the writing framework from page 71 (some children may benefit from this being enlarged to A3).

Stage 5: Writing

Activities:

- Remind children that they are going to continue an explanatory text, writing about another sense.
- Model using your plan to begin some of your paragraphs. Ensure you include the features that you have explored: topic sentences; coordinating conjunctions in report text and subordinating conjunctions in explanations; use of second person to engage the reader and third person to show universality.
- Give children a few minutes to 'talk like a writer' and tell their partner the text as they plan to write it. If it helps, ask them to use a polite 'writer's voice'. Remind them to use their plan and not to invent another text as they go along.
- Let response partners give some brief feedback before children swap roles.
- Tell children your expectations about how much space each part of the story will take up on the page, e.g.
  - Section 1: 4–5 lines
  - Section 2: 5–7 lines
  - Section 3: 3–5 lines.
  (Amend these line numbers for your class and the amount of time they have to write.)
- Read aloud the success criteria (online at My Rising Stars).
- Let the children write. Break up the process. Talk about the focus for each paragraph and quickly model a sentence or idea that the children could try out in their writing.
- Five minutes before the end of the session, ask all children to stop writing and read their story aloud to themselves. If they find errors, or missing words or words they can improve, they should use this opportunity to make changes.

Resources needed:

The success criteria

Each child needs:

- the copy of the text they have previously highlighted and annotated
- the completed mind map
- the flipchart they used for drafting
- the writing framework (or just success criteria for children who will write with more independence).

Stage 6: Improving, editing, reviewing and sharing the writing

Activities:

- Revisit together the success criteria (online at My Rising Stars).
- Model the process below using your work as an example. The children can give you feedback on each step of the process. After you model a step the children have a go with their partner at editing their own work.
- Ask children to reread their texts three times with their response partner:
  - First read through: Children read their partner's text out loud to them. The child who wrote the text listens to check that their writing makes sense, listens out for obvious errors and checks the text follows their plan. Children then swap roles.
  - Second read through: Children read their partner's text and highlight the success criteria they have met. They suggest three places where their partner could improve their work (to achieve or further improve on the success criteria).
  - Third read through: Children proofread their partner's text together with them. They check for errors in punctuation and spelling and correct these as necessary. You should give input at this stage if needed.

Resources needed:

Each child needs:

- the success criteria
- their writing/completed writing framework
- different coloured highlighters/pens/pencils.

Lessons from writing

- Prior to the session, identify errors that were commonly made. Write sample sentences that need to be corrected and ask the children to help you to fix them. These could include:

  o mixing up second and third person, e.g. *You hear though your ears. Your ears can tell you if a sound is loud or soft, familiar or strange. The ears can be damaged by sounds that are too loud so people should be careful what they listen to, especially if you have earphones.*

    - Remind children that the reader needs to know who is being talked about so they can follow ideas through the text.
    - Can children change this to all third person or mostly second person?
    - What is the impact of the change?

  o confused order of events, e.g. *The sound makes the ear drum vibrate. But first it has to go into the ear. Then it goes to the brain. The brain hears the sound. It tells the body how to respond.*

    - *It goes along nerves.* Ask children to number, then to reorder these sentences.
    - Compare their new text with this one. How does it help a reader if the information is in a good order?

Improving the writing

- **After the texts have been marked:** give the children time to read through your comments, to look at the success criteria and to implement any changes suggested. This should not involve the children rewriting the entire text – just those parts that you would like them to revisit to practise/improve their writing.

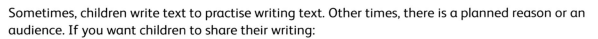

Share

Sometimes, children write text to practise writing text. Other times, there is a planned reason or an audience. If you want children to share their writing:

- they can rewrite it to presentation standard; however, this should be regarded simply as a handwriting activity not as another opportunity to improve the text – the rewritten text should be used for a specific audience or display
- they can make it into pages for a class book on the senses
- they can redraft it into a multi-media presentation.

Name: Class: Date:

General introduction

Say what something is like

Give information about the whole text

What are senses?

Your body has lots of ways of finding out about the world around you. It uses things called senses. You have five main senses. You can touch with your skin, see with your eyes, hear with your ears, taste with your tongue and smell with your nose. You have used one or more of your senses to discover everything you know about the world around you.

Your eyes, ears, skin, nose and tongue send messages to your brain. The messages travel along pathways called nerves. Your brain gets the message and decides what to do.

Subject information

Say what something is like

Give information about the sense Include:

- which part of the body senses the world
- example words showing some things it might sense
- how the body part does the sensing

How does _____ work?

More detailed subject information

Say how or why something happens

Give an example of something happening that involves the sense

List how the sense sends messages to the brain and what happens next

What happens inside the body when we _____ something?

Diagram to match text

Notes on hearing

Sounds go into ear. Hit ear drum. Ear drum vibrates (wobbles). Vibrations travel along nerves to brain. Brain unscrambles vibrations and knows the sound.

Name: Date:

	Contents	Text structure and organisation	Sentence structure	Vocabulary and descriptions	Punctuation	Spelling and handwriting
Working **at greater depth within** the expected standard	Topic sentences are used to introduce paragraphs.	Paragraphs are generally used to group related ideas. The diagram supports the organisation of text.	Appropriate choice of pronouns is used to avoid repetition. Standard English verb inflections are used (e.g. *I was, we were,* etc.).	More sophisticated vocabulary is used. Noun phrases may be expanded with prepositional phrases.	Apostrophes, if used, are used accurately.	Spelling changes needed to add vowel suffixes are often accurate. In handwriting, most letters are appropriately joined or word-processing speed is developing and does not impede thought processes.
Working **at** the expected standard	An explanatory report about the senses is written.	Paragraphs are often used to group related ideas. Sequence of events is explained in a logical order. More general information is given before specific information.	Second person pronouns/determiner are used to engage the reader; third person pronouns/determiners are used to show universality. Present tense is used throughout. Coordinating conjunctions (e.g. *and, or, but*) are used to link ideas. Subordinating conjunctions (e.g. *because, when, until*) are used to add information and to explain.	Specific technical vocabulary is appropriate to the topic. Expanded noun phrases are used to describe and specify.	Question marks are used at the end of a question. Most sentences are punctuated with a full stop. Commas may be used to separate items in lists.	A range of suffixes and prefixes is used. Taught spellings from the Year 3/4 word list are correct. Some letters are joined using diagonal or horizontal strokes. Letters and spaces are in proportion to each other.
Working **towards** the expected standard	The text follows the plan.	Ideas are grouped appropriately.	At least two different conjunctions are used correctly. Most of the text is in the present tense.	Topic-related vocabulary is used. A few noun phrases are expanded with adjectives.	End of sentence punctuation (.?!) is often accurate.	Spelling errors are phonetically decodable. Spaces between letters and words allow for good legibility.

Garden Creatures

Do you ever play in a garden? That garden is part of the biggest nature reserve in Britain. In the UK, we have over 16,000,000 (16 million) gardens. We like to think of our gardens as our private property but, whether we like it or not, we share them with masses of wildlife.

You may think your garden is empty of birds, frogs and hedgehogs, but every garden contains thousands of different types of insects, spiders, woodlice and slugs. You might not like them, or even notice them, but these small creatures are really important as they provide food for the bigger creatures we like to see.

Why are hedgehogs our favourite animal?

Have you ever seen a hedgehog? They have been voted as the UK's favourite animal, possibly because they always look like they are smiling.

Hedgehogs are shy creatures and they are very good at hiding so they are more common in gardens than people think.

Hedgehogs usually come out at night. They snuffle around our lawns and flowerbeds to hunt for their favourite foods: worms and slugs. Hedgehogs use their whiskers, together with their sense of smell, to find their food.

Hedgehogs like to live in gardens with bushes, hedges, compost bins or log piles so that they can sleep during the day and hibernate in winter.

Are squirrels pests or a pleasure?

Have you seen a squirrel scampering in your garden? The American grey squirrel is common in gardens throughout the UK. The British native red squirrel is now only seen in Scotland and in a few other parts of the UK because grey squirrels are more aggressive and have driven the red squirrels out.

A rare red squirrel in Scotland.

Some people don't like grey squirrels because they strip the bark from trees, looking for insects hiding underneath. They also take food from bird feeders. However, they are funny, entertaining and great acrobats. Grey squirrels can live almost anywhere, as long as there are some trees they can scamper into if they sense danger.

Grey squirrels take shelter in trees if they sense danger.

Unit 7: Garden Creatures

Name: Class: Date:

1. What shares our gardens with us?

   _____

2. Tick **two** facts from the text that are true about insects, spiders, woodlice and slugs.

   No one likes them because they eat plants.   ☐

   There are thousands of them in every garden.   ☐

   They keep the birds, frogs and hedgehogs away.   ☐

   They provide food for bigger creatures.   ☐

3. Why is it hard to know if you have a hedgehog in your garden?

   _____

4. Why do hedgehogs like gardens with bushes or log piles?

   _____

5. Why are most people in England more likely to see an American grey squirrel than a British red one?

   _____

6. List **one** reason why people don't like grey squirrels and **one** reason why they do like them.

Don't like them	Do like them

Unit 7 Writing a report/information text with longer entries

In this unit children will:

- read a report/information text with longer entries
- write subheadings to identify the focus for paragraphs
- look at how noun phrases are expanded with accurate, technical vocabulary
- identify present tense forms of verbs
- identify coordinating and subordinating conjunctions and discuss their function and impact
- plan, draft, edit and improve an information/report text.

Stage 1: Responding to the text 📖

Activities:

- Establish prior knowledge.
- *Think, pair, share:* Ask pairs of children to list creatures that live in parks, gardens and outdoor spaces. They can use information from first-hand experience, books or visual media. Ask them to consider:
  - birds
  - mammals, reptiles and amphibians (live on land and water)
  - insects and minibeasts.
- Ask children to jot down something interesting they know about each of their creatures.
- *Snowball* the activity:
  - Let each pair choose their top five creatures and share them with another pair.
  - Then let each group of four agree their top five creatures and share with another four.
  - Ask each group of eight to agree five favourite creatures to share with the class.
- What do children remember about information/report texts that tell about how things are now? List expectations of a text called 'Garden Creatures', e.g.
  - non-fiction text – an information text, not a story
  - it will tell the reader about creatures that live in gardens
  - it may have headings, paragraphs and fact boxes.
- Show the children the text: without reading it, what are the layout clues that it's non-fiction? (E.g. *headings, photographs.*)
- Before reading the text, ensure the children understand the meaning of the more unusual words and phrases: "*nature reserve*", "*private property*", "*wildlife*", "*notice*", "*common*", "*hibernate*", "*native*", "*aggressive*", "*strip the bark*", "*acrobats*" and "*scamper*".
- Help the children remember the meanings of these words by putting them in contextualising sentences, e.g. *We see smartphones everywhere – they have become very common.*
- Read and talk about the text.
  - Were the expectations of the features of non-fiction texts accurate?
  - Can the children add anything else to their list of features? (E.g. *present tense.*)
  - What did the children find out from this text that they didn't know before?

Resources needed:

Shared copy of the text (PDF/IWB/visualiser)

Each child needs:

- a copy of the text
- a copy of the comprehension questions.

- Ask children to answer the reading comprehension questions to ensure close reading of the text and good understanding.
- Together, share answers to the questions and discuss the strategies children used to answer them.

Stage 2: Analysing the text structure and organisation

Activities:

- Ask children to read the text aloud to a response partner to revisit the text, develop fluency, ensure appropriate pronunciation of all words and to practise reading with good intonation and expression.
- Ask children to underline any new words or phrases. Take feedback and explain what these mean in context.

Discussing paragraphs

- Talk first about the headings.
  - Why do you think they are written as questions? (E.g. *To make people want to read the answer, even if they already know about the creature.*)
  - What do they tell us? (E.g. *They tell us which creature the text is going to be about.*)
  - How do they make the text easier to read? (E.g. *By telling the reader what each section is about.*)
  - Why isn't there a heading for each paragraph? (E.g. *Because headings are used for each creature and there is more than one paragraph about each of the creatures.*)
- Model reading the first paragraph aloud and work with the children to think of a subheading for the paragraph (e.g. 'Masses of wildlife'; 'Wildlife in our gardens'). Discuss why you chose that information to highlight.
- Ask children to work in pairs.
  - Child 1 reads the next paragraph aloud. Child 2 has to suggest a subheading for the paragraph and write it on a sticky note. The subheading doesn't have to be a question, but it should tell the reader what the paragraph is about.
  - Child 2 reads the next paragraph aloud while child 1 writes a subheading.
  - Continue swapping paragraphs until each has a subheading.
  - Ask children to number their sticky notes to show which paragraph number each refers to.
- Lay out eight sheets of paper, each with a paragraph number.
  - Ask children to stick their sticky notes to the page with the relevant paragraph number.
  - Compare the subheadings. Was there a broad consensus of the topic? Discuss any anomalies.
- Ask children why they think the author didn't give each paragraph its own subheading. (E.g. *The paragraphs are not long enough to need their own subheadings; too many headings and subheadings would make the text too busy and complicated.*)

Discussing organisation

- Ask children to:
  - draw circles around the three sections in the text. (Check their circles match the introduction, hedgehogs and squirrels.)
  - *think, pair, share:*
    - How do we know these are separate sections?
    - Does it matter which order we read them in? (*Yes – we have to read the introduction first. It doesn't matter which order we put the other sections in.*)

Resources needed:

Shared copy of the text (PDF/IWB/ visualiser)

Eight sheets of paper

Each pair needs:

- sticky notes

Each child needs:

- a copy of the text
- highlighters/coloured pencils in four different colours (ideally, same colours for all children).

○ Discuss how the organisation of paragraphs is different in this report/information text from a story. (E.g. *In stories, paragraph order matters because paragraphs usually describe a sequence of events. In a report/ information text like this, there is no need for a particular order. We can call these texts non-chronological which means that they don't have to be read in a particular sequence.*)

Stage 3: Analysing the text purpose and language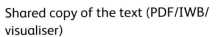

Activities:

Discussing text purpose

- Ask groups of children to reread the text and discuss its purpose. Give them a choice between:
  ○ to tell a story
  ○ to make someone laugh
  ○ to talk about an experience someone had
  ○ to say what something is like.
- Ask groups to think about *how* they know the purpose of the text. Ask them to consider the meaning/contents of the text (e.g. *it tells us about creatures in gardens*).
- Ask them to discuss the purpose of layout features including:
  ○ introduction (e.g. *it tells you about all the wildlife that you can see or is hidden in gardens*)
  ○ headings (e.g. *so you know which creature the paragraphs are talking about*)
  ○ paragraphs (e.g. *they group ideas around a topic*)
  ○ photographs (e.g. *they show you what the creature looks like*).

Resources needed:

Shared copy of the text (PDF/IWB/ visualiser)

Each pair needs:
- an enlarged copy of the text

Each child needs:
- the copy of the text
- marker pens/coloured pencils.

Discussing vocabulary

- Ask children to find the words "*snuffle*" and "*scamper*" in the text. Which animal snuffles? Which scampers? Could the verbs be swapped over? Discuss the fact that we have verbs which are very specific to describe the way that animals move.
- Write the words *pounce, prowl, scuttle, flit, crawl, flutter, bound, waddle, slither, leap.* Can children suggest animals that do each of these verbs?
- Can children think of verbs to describe the sounds animals make? (E.g. *Bark, meow, snuffle, snort.*)
- Talk about why it can be useful to use these specific verbs in a non-fiction text.

Discussing language

- Ask children to look for questions in the text.
  ○ What can they tell you about where questions occur in the text? (E.g. *They're in headings and opening sentences of each section.*)
  ○ Why do you think the author used questions in these places? (E.g. *To make people feel that the text is talking to them; to make them want to read on to find the answer.*)
- *Think, pair, share:* Is this text written in the past or present tense? (*Present.*)
- How do you know? (E.g. *Look at the verbs such as "are", "do", "can".*)
- Allocate different pairs of children to different paragraphs and ask them to underline present tense verbs.
  ○ Paragraph 1: 'do', 'is', 'have', 'like', 'think', 'share'
  ○ Paragraph 2: 'may', 'think', 'is', 'contains', 'might', 'like', 'notice', 'are', 'provide', 'see'
  ○ Paragraph 3: 'have', 'look', 'are'
  ○ Paragraph 4: 'are', 'think'
  ○ Paragraph 5: 'come', 'use', 'hunt', 'use', 'find'

- o Paragraph 6: 'like', 'live', 'can', 'sleep', 'hibernate'
- o Paragraph 7: 'have', 'is', 'are'
- o Paragraph 8: 'like', 'strip', 'take', 'are', 'can live', 'scamper', 'sense'.
- Why is the text in the present tense? (E.g. *Because it describes what something is like now*.)
- Draw children's attention to the use of the present perfect tense in questions and sentences such as:
  - o "*Have you … seen?*"; "*They have been voted*"; "*they have driven*" Ask children to find another way of saying each of the clauses (e.g. *Did you see?; They were voted; they drove*). Point out that the rewritten forms use the past tense whereas the present perfect looks like it is using present tense verbs.
  - o Talk about why the writer may have chosen to use present perfect forms instead of past tenses (e.g. *because the rest of the text is in the present tense so it seems to fit better to use a present perfect*).
- Can children tell you which kinds of words are used to link words, ideas and clauses together? (*Conjunctions*.) Allocate pairs of children to a different paragraph. Give them a list of conjunctions and ask them to see which ones they can find in their paragraph: *and, as, as long as, because, but, or, so, so that, if*.
  - o Paragraph 1: 'but'
  - o Paragraph 2: 'but', 'or', 'but', 'as'
  - o Paragraph 3: 'because'
  - o Paragraph 4: 'and', 'so'
  - o Paragraph 5: [none]
  - o Paragraph 6: 'or', 'so that'
  - o Paragraph 7: 'and', 'because', 'and'
  - o Paragraph 8: 'because', 'and', 'as long as', 'if'.
- Ask children to ring the coordinating conjunctions (which link ideas) and underline the subordinating conjunctions (which add more information). Which are there more of in this text? (*Coordinating conjunctions*.) Why? (E.g. *subordinating conjunctions offer explanations and these are less used in report/information texts*.)

Stage 4: Planning to write: Writing a report/information text with longer entries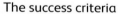

- Prior to the session, decide what you'd like the children to write an information report about. The given one is 'Bees', but you can easily amend it to fit in with a curriculum topic for which children have done some research.

Activities:

- Tell the children they are going to be writing an information report about 'Bees'.
- Give children time to research bees using appropriate non-fiction books or the internet.
- *Think, pair, share:* Ask children to list anything they know about or have found out about bees.
  - o *Snowball* the activity: Ask pairs to share with another pair.
  - o Ask each group of four to choose their five best bee facts to share with another four.
  - o Ask each group of eight to choose their five best bee facts to share with the class.
- Distribute the writing framework.
  - o Model identifying bee facts from the information provided that could go in the same paragraph. Do children know other information that could be grouped into the same paragraph?
  - o Ask children to work in pairs to agree which of the other bee facts would go together in the same paragraph. They should highlight/underline to indicate their decisions.

Resources needed:

Shared copy of the text (PDF/IWB/visualiser)

The success criteria

Groups of children need:

- a flipchart/large paper and marker pens
- access to the internet or relevant non-fiction books about bees for research

Each child needs:

- the copy of the text they have previously highlighted and annotated
- the writing framework from page 82 (some children may benefit from this being enlarged to A3)
- highlighters/pens/pencils.

- o Challenge them to add at least two more facts from their research. Will they need to add another paragraph to accommodate these new facts?
- Look together at the headings in the model text. Ask children to think of questions as headings for their sections on bees.
- Using the information you linked earlier, say aloud a paragraph for the children to respond to.
- Ask children to write subheadings for the paragraphs they identified. Model the process for the facts you linked earlier. Remind them of the way they did this at Stage 2 (above).
- Let children talk through their ideas for their text with a different response partner who can indicate whether the text makes sense.
- Give each child the opportunity to 'talk like a writer' to a different response partner, to rehearse the structure and language of their text and to receive peer feedback.
- Ask the children to decide what a successful information text should include. Compare this to the success criteria (online at My Rising Stars) and amend if necessary.
- Clarify the success criteria.

Stage 5: Writing ▭ ✏

Activities:

- Model turning your plan into a paragraph. Ensure you use the features identified in your success criteria and in the writing framework, and include present tense verbs (including the present perfect), specific vocabulary, use of conjunctions to join ideas, headings to introduce the main idea of sections and text paragraphs to group information.
- Give children a few minutes to 'talk like a writer' and orally rehearse the text as they plan to write it. If it helps, ask them to use a polite 'writer's voice'. Remind them to use their plan and not to invent another text as they go along.
- Let response partners give some brief feedback before children swap roles.
- Tell children your expectations about how much space each part of the text will take up on the page, e.g.
  - o Introduction: 2–3 lines
  - o Each bee: 6–8 lines (this should include more than one paragraph about each bee).
  (Amend these line numbers for your class and the amount of time they have to write.)
- Remind children they can compose and rehearse sentences inside their head or in a low whisper before they begin to write them.
- Read aloud the success criteria (online at My Rising Stars).
- Let the children write. Break up the process so the children remain in control of what they are writing. Talk about the focus for each paragraph and quickly model a sentence or idea that the children could try out in their writing.
- Five minutes before the end of the stage, ask all children to stop writing and read their story aloud to themselves. If they find errors, or missing words or words they can improve, they should use this opportunity to make changes.

Resources needed:

The success criteria

Each child needs:

- the copy of the text they have previously highlighted and annotated
- the completed writing framework
- a PC/laptop/tablet if the children are word-processing.

Stage 6: Improving, editing, reviewing and sharing the writing

Activities:

- Revisit together the success criteria (online at My Rising Stars).
- Model the process below using your work as an example. The children can give you feedback on each step of the process. After you model a step, the children should have a go with their partner at editing their own work.

Resources needed:

The success criteria
Each child needs:

- their writing/completed writing framework
- different coloured highlighters/pens.

- Ask children to reread their texts three times with their response partner:
  - First read through: Children read their partner's text out loud to them. The child who wrote the text listens to check that their writing makes sense, listens out for obvious errors and checks the text follows their plan. Children then swap roles.
  - Second read through: Children read their partner's text and highlight the success criteria they have met. They suggest three places where their partner could improve their work (to achieve or further improve on the success criteria).
  - Third read through: Children proofread their partner's text together with them. They check for errors in punctuation and spelling and correct these as necessary. You should give input at this stage if needed.

Lessons from writing

- Prior to the session, identify errors that were commonly made. Write sample sentences that need to be corrected and ask the children to help you to fix them. These could include:
  - muddled information in the same paragraph, e.g. *Bees live in large groups. They do a waggle-dance to tell other bees where to find nectar. There is only one queen bee in each hive. They use the nectar to make honey to eat.*
    - Ask children to identify which statements do belong together and to cross out the statements that belong elsewhere in the text. Remind them that paragraphs should be used to provide linked information.
  - inconsistent use of tense, e.g. *Bumble bees are big bees. They don't live in hives so in the winter they were cold. Also there were not many flowers so the bumble bees couldn't get the nectar. Bumble bees feed on nectar so they don't need to make honey.*
    - Ask children to identify the errors and clarify that most information report texts are written in the present tense.

Improving the writing

After the texts have been marked: give the children time to read through your comments, to look at the success criteria and to implement any changes suggested. This should not involve the children rewriting the entire text – just those parts that you would like them to revisit to practise/improve their writing.

Share

Sometimes, children write text to practise writing text. Other times, there is a planned reason or an audience. If you want children to share their writing:

- appoint 'editors' for a class magazine called 'Bee-keeping; let your editors choose sentences or paragraphs from each child's work – the individual children can then polish or improve the section of their work for the magazine
- let children collect and collate images and video of their bees and use their text as an audio track to an online presentation.

| Name: | | Class: | Date: |

Sort or colour the facts below to show how you will group them into paragraphs in your text about bees.

Bumble bees	Honey bees
• Big bees	• Live in large groups
• Don't live in hives	• Collect nectar and pollen from flowers in nearby gardens
• 24 different types live in UK	• Use waggle-dance to tell other bees where to find nectar
• Don't make much honey	• Colour warns animals to leave them alone
• Usually gentle but can sting	• Use nectar to make honey as food
• Gather pollen on their legs and spread it from flower to flower quickly	• One hive can have over 50,000 worker bees
• Live in underground burrows in family groups of up to 400	• Only one queen bee to a hive
• Large, fuzzy with black and yellow bands	• Spread pollen as they visit different flowers
• Feed on nectar from flowers	• Will sting if threatened
Add new information here	**Add new information here**

Think of some possible headings you could use.

Bumble bees	Honey bees

Name: Date:

	Contents	Text structure and organisation	Sentence structure	Vocabulary and descriptions	Punctuation	Spelling and handwriting
Working at greater depth within the expected standard	Additional information is added and embedded from independent research.	The text is logically organised. Topic sentences introduce each paragraph.	Appropriate choice of pronouns is used to avoid repetition. Standard English verb inflections are used (e.g. I was, we were, etc.).	More sophisticated vocabulary is used. Noun phrases may be extended with prepositional phrases.		Spelling changes needed to add vowel suffixes are often accurate. In handwriting, most letters are appropriately joined or word-processing speed is developing and does not impede thought processes.
Working at the expected standard	An information/report text about bees is written.	Paragraphs are used to group related ideas. A short introduction gives an overview of the topic.	Each paragraph is about a different topic. The present tense is used throughout. Coordinating conjunctions (e.g. and, or, but) are used to link ideas. Subordinating conjunctions (e.g. because, when, until) are used to add information.	Specific technical vocabulary about bees is used appropriately. Some expanded noun phrases are used to describe and specify	Question marks are used at the end of a question. Most sentences are punctuated with a full stop. Commas may be used to separate items in lists.	A range of suffixes and prefixes is used. Taught spellings from the Year 3/4 word list are correct. Some letters are joined using diagonal or horizontal strokes. Letters and spaces are in proportion to each other.
Working towards the expected standard	The text follows the plan.	Ideas are grouped appropriately.	At least two different conjunctions are used correctly. Most of the text is in the present tense.	Topic-related vocabulary is used.	End of sentence punctuation (.?!) is often accurate. Apostrophes are used for contractions (missing letters).	Spelling errors are phonetically decodable. Spaces between letters and words allow for good legibility.

The Stick Book: Loads of things you can make or do with a stick

Jo Schofield and Fiona Danks

Go outside and find a stick. Choose your stick carefully and it can be anything: a toy for a dog, the start of a craft or science project, a musical instrument, the beginning of a tent or a campfire, a game to play with friends, a magic wand or anything else your imagination allows it to be.

Make a flying machine

On a windy day, try transforming a pile of sticks, paper, sticky tape and card into flying machines.

Go to an open hillside or field (make sure it's not near a road) for a flying competition. Whose plane can fly highest and furthest? Who can come up with the most impressive or the wackiest design?

- Tape two straight sticks together in a cross: one for the body of your machine and the other for the front edge of the wings.
- The rest of the design is up to you, but here are a few tips. Make wings from a plastic bag, paper, garden fleece or some other lightweight material. The wings must be large enough to lift the plane into the air. Stick them in place with a small amount of tape. Cut out tail flights from thin cardboard or a plastic milk container. Stick a small weight (e.g. clay or a small pebble) on the machine's nose.

Make a sun clock

Use a stick to tell the time for a day and see how the earth moves in relation to the sun. Make sure you have a clock or watch handy.

- Find an open area of ground that gets the sun all day – perhaps a beach (preferably above the high-tide line), a playground, a lawn or a patio. If you plan to keep your sun clock in that spot, make sure you use a place where it won't be disturbed.

- In the morning, push a straight 1 m/3 ft stick into the ground in the centre of the open area or, if you're using a site with a hard surface, place it in a plant pot. Make sure the stick is vertical.

- Every hour on the hour mark the tip of the stick's shadow with a short stick or a pebble, writing the number of the hour beside it if you wish!

- As, towards winter, the sun moves lower in the sky the shadows will change.

Unit 8: The Stick Book: Loads of things you can make or do with a stick

Name: Class: Date:

1. Draw lines to match the material to the part it could be on a flying machine.

    Material   *Part of the flying machine*

    (stick)   (tail flight)

    (garden fleece)   (front edge of wing)

    (milk container)   (wing)

2. Why would you need big wings on your flying machine?

    _____

3. What is the last thing you need to do when you make a flying machine?

    _____

4. Why should you have a clock or watch handy when you make a sun clock?

    _____

5. Why might you need a plant pot to make a stick sun clock?

    _____

6. List all the things you would need to follow these instructions and make a sun clock.

    _____

    _____

Unit 8 Writing an instructional text

In this unit children will:

- read an instructional text
- discuss structure and clarify expectations of paragraphs which introduce each set of instructions
- identify features of second person writing including pronouns and verb forms
- recognise the importance of adverbs in instructional texts and identify coordinating conjunctions
- consider different ways of expanding noun phrases and the importance of precise vocabulary
- plan, draft, edit and improve an instructional text.

Stage 1: Responding to the text

Activities:

- Show the children your sticks. Discuss where they came from.
- In groups, ask them to think about what you could make or do with sticks like these if you also had paper, card, sticky tape, string, etc. as well as things you can find outside. Ask children to:
  - talk about their ideas
  - sketch ideas on large sheets of paper, labelling materials
  - look at sketches made by other groups and talk about good ideas.
- What do children remember about instructional texts that tell you how to make or do something? List expectations of a text called 'Loads of things you can make or do with a stick', e.g.
  - non-fiction text – an information text, not a story
  - it will tell you how to make or do things
  - it will have command (imperative) verbs
  - it may have headings, lists and pictures.
- Show the children the text; without reading it, what are the layout clues that it's non-fiction? (E.g. *headings, photographs, bullet points*.)
- Before reading the text, ensure the children understand the meaning of the more unusual words and phrases: "*transforming*", "*wackiest*", "*tail flights*", "*disturbed*" and "*vertical*". Help the children remember the meanings of these words by putting them in contextualising sentences, e.g. *When we cook a cake we transform eggs, sugar, butter and flour into something new and delicious!*
- Read and talk about the text.
  - Were the expectations of the features of instructional texts accurate?
  - Can the children add anything else to their list of features? (E.g. *Present tense.*)
  - Do they think they have enough information to make or do these things?

Resources needed:

Shared copy of the text (PDF/IWB/ visualiser)

Some sticks from an outdoor space

Each group needs:

- large paper.

Each child needs:

- a copy of the text
- a copy of the comprehension questions.

- Ask the children to answer the reading comprehension questions to ensure close reading of the text and good understanding.
- Together, share answers to the questions and discuss the strategies children used to answer them. Look at question 6 together and share strategies for locating information quickly and accurately.

Stage 2: Analysing the text structure and organisation

Activities:

- Ask children to read the text aloud to a response partner to revisit the text, develop fluency, ensure appropriate pronunciation of all words and to practise reading with good intonation and expression.
- Ask children to underline any new words or phrases. Take feedback and explain what these mean in context.

Resources needed:

Shared copy of the text (PDF/IWB/visualiser)

Each pair needs:
- an enlarged copy of the text
- a pair of scissors.

Each child needs:
- a copy of the text
- highlighters/pens/coloured pencils (each child/pair needs the same three colours).

Discussing text structure

- Model the activities below on one of the paragraphs to ensure that children have a clear understanding of each point.
- Ask children to:
  - use one colour to underline headings (*"Make a flying machine"; "Make a sun clock"*)
  - use another colour to circle introductions to each section (*paragraphs beginning "On a windy day"; "Use a stick to tell the time for a day"*)
  - use a different colour to circle the instructions for each activity.
- *Think pair, share:*
  - How do we know there are separate sections? (*They have different headings.*)
  - Does it matter which order we read the section in? (*We should read the opening paragraph first, but after that it doesn't matter.*)
  - Does it matter which order we read the bullet points in? (*Yes.*) Why? (*The instructions are written in the order they need to be carried out. They are in chronological order – the sequence matters.*)

Discussing paragraphs

- *Think pair, share:* Distribute the enlarged copy of the text and ask the children how many introductory paragraphs they can identify. (*Three.*)
  - Where are they? (*A general one at the beginning and one at the beginning of each section.*)
  - How are they different from other paragraphs? (E.g. *They tell you where to go; they tell you what you can do when you've made something; the first introduction tells you all kinds of things you can make with a stick; all the other paragraphs are instruction or information so they are often shorter.*)
- In their pairs, ask children to cut up the text into separate paragraphs.
  - Without comparing it to the original, can they reconstruct the original paragraph order, paragraph by paragraph?
  - While they're working, ask them to think about the clues they are using.
  - Discuss the clues the children used (e.g. *the text makes sense in this order; the introduction has to come first in each section*).

Stage 3: Analysing the text purpose and language

Activities:

Discussing text purpose

- Ask groups of children to reread the text and discuss its purpose. Give them a choice between:
  - to tell someone how to do something
  - to make someone laugh
  - to talk about an experience someone had
  - to say what something is like.
- Ask groups to think about *how* they know the purpose of the text.
- Together, make a list of all the organisational features children would expect to see in an instruction text (encourage them to think beyond this text to other instructional texts they have read), e.g.
  - a statement telling you what you're going to do or make
  - a list, often with pictures, of things you need
  - a list of what to do
  - a photograph of what you're trying to make
  - numbers for the instructions
  - adverbs like *First, Next, Then, Finally* could be used to confirm the order of the instructions.
- Model looking at this text for some of the features.
- *Think, pair, share:* Look at this text. Which of the features from the list can you spot here?
- Together discuss why the authors included some features and why they might not have included others.

Discussing verbs and person

- Ask children what they know about command (imperative) verbs which are found in instructions (e.g. *they don't have a word/pronoun like* you *in front of them; they're usually at the beginning of a sentence, or after an adverb*).
- Allocate pairs of children to a different section from last time and ask them to find imperative (command) verbs:
  - Introduction paragraph (*'Go', 'Choose'*)
  - Flying machine text (*'Make', 'try', 'tape', 'make', 'stick', 'cut', 'stick'*)
  - Sun clock text (*'Make', 'Use', 'see', 'Make', 'find', 'make sure', 'push', 'place', 'Make sure', 'mark'*).
- Ask them why they think this text has so many of these verbs. (*It's telling you what to do.*)
- Remind children that:
  - some texts are written from the writer's point of view and use words such as (pronouns) *I, me, mine* and (possessive determiner) *my* – we say that these texts are written in the first person
  - some texts talk directly to the reader and use words such as (pronouns) *you, yours* and (possessive determiner) *your* – we say that these texts are written in the second person
  - some texts are talking about something or someone and use words such as (pronouns) *it, she, they* and (possessive determiners) *her, its, their* – we say that these texts are written in the third person.
- Ask children to look at the text and identify whether they think it's mostly written in the first, second or third person. (*Second.*)
- Clarify that instructions speak directly to the reader by using command/imperative verbs and pronouns like *you* and possessive determiners like *your.*

Resources needed:

Shared copy of the text (PDF/IWB/visualiser)

Each pair needs:

- an enlarged copy of the text.

Each child needs:

- a copy of the text
- marker pens/coloured pencils.

Discussing language

- Do children remember the information adverbs give them? (*How, when or where the action is carried out.*)
  - Ask children to underline all the adverbial phrases (e.g. *'on a windy day'*, *'in the morning'*, *'every hour on the hour'*). Explain that adverbs can identify:
    - *when* to do something (e.g. *'First'*, *'Then'*, *'Next'*, *'Finally'*, *'First thing in the morning'*, *'Now'*)
    - *how* to do something (e.g. *'carefully'*, *'how'*).
- Allocate pairs of children to different sections and ask them to look for conjunctions:
  - Introduction paragraph (*'and'*, *'or'*)
  - Flying machine text (*'and'*, *'or'*)
  - Sun clock text (*'and'*, *'if'*, *'or'*).
- Ask them why they don't find conjunctions such as *because or so* in a text like this (e.g. *it's not aiming to explain why things happen, just to tell you what to do*).
- *Think, pair, share:* Is this text written in the past or present tense? (*Present.*)
  - How do you know? (E.g. *Look at the verbs. All command verbs are present tense.*)
  - Can children find other present tense verbs? (E.g. *'find'*, *'can'*, *'be'*, *'to play'*, *'allows'*, *'to be'*, *'can fly'*, *'can come'*, *'must be'*, *'to lift'*, *'see'*, *'moves'*, *'have'*, *'gets'*, *'plan'*, *'to keep'*, *'use'*, *'be'*, *'are using'*, *'can'*, *'wish'*, *'to tell'*.)
  - Why is the text in the present tense? (E.g. *Because it tells you what to do as you do it.*)
- Can children identify adjectives in noun phrases? (E.g. *'Musical'*, *'magic'*, *'open'*, *'sticky'*, *'flying'*, *'most impressive'*, *'wackiest'*, *'plastic'*, *'lightweight'*, *'thin'*, *'small'*, *'straight'*, *'hard'*, *'plant'*.)
- Talk about the function of these adjectives. Clarify that:
  - if it's important to distinguish, e.g. a straight stick from a crooked one, or a hard surface from a soft one, then adjectives are included in expanded noun phrases
  - adjectives in this text are *not* intended to create an image in the reader's mind.
- Introduce another way of extending a noun phrase: by adding a prepositional phrase. Tell children that a prepositional phrase is formed of a preposition (e.g. *from, of, with*) followed by another noun phrase.
  - Point out the noun phrases "*a toy <u>for</u> a dog*"; "*the body <u>of</u> your machine*"; "*the front edge <u>of</u> the wings*"; "*wings <u>from</u> a plastic bag*". Can children identify the preposition in the middle of them?
  - Give children a list of prepositions that introduce prepositional phrases used to expand noun phrases and see how many they can find and underline. Ask them to look for: "*for*", "*from*", "*on*", "*of*", "*with*".
  - Ask children to look at the prepositions they have underlined. Are there any that could be replaced by an adjective or could be expressed differently?

Stage 4: Planning to write: Writing an instructional text

- Prior to the session, decide on what you'd like the children to write as an instructional text. The given one is 'games with sticks', but you can easily amend it to fit in with a curriculum topic for which children have done some research.

Activities:

- Tell the children they are going to be writing an instructional text about games with sticks.
- Working in groups, ask children to list games they know that involve sticks (e.g. *Pooh sticks, relay races, hockey, throwing sticks like spears to see who can throw the furthest, quoits, pick-up sticks*).

Resources needed:

Shared copy of the text (PDF/IWB/visualiser)

The success criteria

Groups of children need:

- some garden/park/outdoor sticks
- a flipchart/large paper and marker pens.

Each child needs:

- the copy of the text they have previously highlighted and annotated
- the writing framework from page 93 (some children may benefit from this being enlarged to A3).

- Give each group a few sticks and ask them to work together to create a game using one or more sticks.
  - It can be a version/variation of a known game.
  - It can be a completely new game.
  - It must involve one or more sticks. The sticks can be of any tree, length and strength.
  - Once children have described their game to each other, ask them to play the game, or to mime playing it so that all group members know and understand the game's structure.
- Distribute the writing framework.
- Model using the plan to show how to play a game like Pooh sticks.
  - Ask children to work in pairs to answer the questions and to draw a diagram of the game being played. They may need to confer with other members of their group.
- Let children talk through their plan with a response partner from a different group who can indicate whether the instructions make sense.
- Give each child the opportunity to 'talk like a writer' to a different response partner to rehearse the structure and language of their text and to receive peer feedback.
- Ask children to decide what a successful instructional text will look like and amend success criteria (online at My Rising Stars) if necessary.
- Clarify the success criteria.

Stage 5: Writing

Activities:

- Remind children that they are going to write an instruction text about games with sticks.
- Model using your plan to write an introduction and some of your instructions. Ensure you include features from the success criteria, e.g. imperative verbs, second person pronouns/possessive determiners, adverbs (where necessary to show order or manner), chronological order, clear precise sentences, noun phrases expanded with accurate adjectives/prepositional phrases.

Resources needed:

The success criteria

Each child needs:

- the copy of the text they have previously highlighted and annotated
- the completed writing framework.

- Give children a few minutes to 'talk like a writer' and orally rehearse the text as they plan to write it. If it helps, ask them to use a polite 'writer's voice'. Remind them to use their plan.
- Let response partners give some brief feedback before children swap roles.
- Tell children your expectations about how much space each part of the story will take up on the page, e.g.
  - Introduction: 2–3 lines
  - Instructions: 18–20 lines.

  (Amend these line numbers for your class and the amount of time they have to write.)
- Remind children they can compose and rehearse sentences inside their head or in a low whisper before they begin to write them.
- Read aloud the success criteria (online at My Rising Stars).
- Let the children write. Break up the process. Talk about the focus for each paragraph and quickly model a sentence or idea that the children could try out in their writing.
- Five minutes before the end of the stage, ask all children to stop writing and read their story aloud to themselves. If they find errors, missing words or words they can improve, they should use this opportunity to make changes.

Stage 6: Improving, editing, reviewing and sharing the writing

Activities:

- Revisit together the success criteria (online at My Rising Stars).
- Model the process below using your work as an example. The children can give you feedback on each step of the process. After you model a step, the children should have a go with their partner at editing their own work.

Resources needed:

Each child needs:

- the success criteria
- their writing/completed writing framework
- different coloured highlighters/pens.

- Ask children to reread their texts three times with their response partner:
  - First read through: Children read their partner's text out loud to them. The child who wrote the text listens to check that their writing makes sense, listens out for obvious errors and checks the text follows their plan. Children then swap roles.
  - Second read through: Children read their partner's text and highlight the success criteria they have met. They suggest three places where their partner could improve their work (to achieve or further improve on the success criteria).
  - Third read through: Children proofread their partner's text together with them. They check for errors in punctuation and spelling and correct these as necessary. You should give input at this stage if needed.

Lessons from writing

- Prior to the session, identify errors that were commonly made. Write sample sentences that need to be corrected and ask the children to help you to fix them. These could include:
  - muddled order, e.g. *Throw your sticks into the water but first stand on a bridge. Run across the bridge to see the winner. The stick that comes out first is the winner.*
    - Together unscramble this order. Explain that one reason for planning and reading through the text is so that the order is clear. Make sure children know how to indicate text out of order in their writing – we all forget things sometimes.
  - using too many sentences when an extended noun phrase would be more helpful, e.g. *Get your sticks. Get the paper. Make it into a kite shape. Tape them on.*
    - Can children put all of this information about making a kite into one sentence (E.g. *Tape your sticks onto the kite-shaped paper.*)? Emphasise the need for precise and concise language in instructions.

Improving the writing

- **After the texts have been marked:** give the children time to read through your comments, to look at the success criteria and to implement any changes suggested. This should not involve the children rewriting the entire text – just those parts that you would like them to revisit to practise/improve their writing.

Share

Sometimes, children write text to practise writing text. Other times, there is a planned reason or an audience. If you want children to share their writing:

- capture digital photographs of children preparing for and playing their game; let children create presentation texts to accompany each of the pictures – publish the texts in a book of 'Games to play with Sticks'
- let children video themselves preparing for and playing the game then use their text as an audio instruction to accompany the video.

Unit 8: Writing an instructional text

Name: Class: Date:

Planning to write instructions for playing a game with a stick or sticks

Name of game: _____

Number of players: _____   Age of players: _____

Equipment needed: _____

_____

What needs to be done before the game starts? _____

_____

_____

_____

Labelled diagram of players playing the game:

```
┌─────────────────────────────────────────────────────┐
│                                                       │
│                                                       │
│                                                       │
│                                                       │
│                                                       │
│                                                       │
│                                                       │
│                                                       │
│                                                       │
│                                                       │
│                                                       │
│                                                       │
└─────────────────────────────────────────────────────┘
```

How will you know who the winner is? _____

_____

_____

_____

_____

_____

Unit 8: Moderating writing: Writing an instructional text

Name: Date:

	Contents	Text structure and organisation	Sentence structure	Vocabulary and descriptions	Punctuation	Spelling and handwriting
Working **at greater depth within** the expected standard	Instructions are clear and easy to follow.	The text is logically organised with an introduction followed by instructions. Additional useful information may be included.	Concise sentences are used to give clear instructions. The text includes at least three different types of sentence.	Noun phrases may be expanded with prepositional phrases.		Spelling changes needed to add vowel suffixes are often accurate. In handwriting, most letters are appropriately joined or word-processing speed is developing and does not impede thought processes.
Working **at** the expected standard	A coherent sequence of instructions is given. An introductory paragraph to explain the desired outcome is included.	Paragraphs are used to group sentences relating to the same stage of an instruction. Heading indicates the aim of the instructions (e.g. *How to, To make,* etc.)	Some instructions begin with an adverb to indicate sequence. Command (imperative) verb forms are consistently used. Conjunctions (e.g. *or, and, but*) are used to link ideas. Second person pronouns/possessive determiners are used consistently.	Noun phrases are expanded with informative adjectives. All vocabulary is specific and explicit so the reader knows what they need.	Most end of sentence punctuation (.?!) is accurate. Bullet points or numbers are used to indicate each instruction.	A range of prefixes and suffixes is used. Taught spellings from the Year 3/4 word list are correct. Some letters are joined using diagonal or horizontal strokes. Letters and spaces are in proportion to each other.
Working **towards** the expected standard	Some instructions are given. A short introduction is included.	Ideas are grouped together.	The text is in the present tense.	Some adjectives are used to create noun phrases.	End of sentence punctuation (.?!) is often accurate.	Spelling errors are phonetically decodable. Spaces between letters and words allow for good legibility.

The Teacher's Day in Bed

David Orme

Our teacher's having a day in bed –
She's sent her pets to school instead!

There's …

A parrot to read the register,
A crocodile to sharpen the pencils,
A canary to teach singing,
An adder to teach maths,
An octopus to make the ink,
An elephant to hoover the floor,
An electric eel to make the computer work,
A giraffe to look for trouble at the back,
A tiger to keep order at the front,
A reed bunting (can't you guess?
to help with reading, of course!),
A secretary bird to run the office
A piranha fish to give swimming lessons
(Glad I'm off swimming today!),
A zebra to help with crossing the road,
Oh, and a dragon to cook the sausages.

I bet that none of you ever knew
Just how many things a teacher can do!

Unit 9: The Teacher's Day in Bed

Name: **Class:**   **Date:**

1. Why is an adder a good pet to teach maths?

   _____

2. Do you think children will misbehave in this class?

   Explain why, using ideas from the poem.

   _____

3. A reed bunting is a small bird. What does the poem say it could do in school?

   _____

4. Why is the narrator pleased not to be in swimming lessons?

   _____

5. Draw lines to match the pets to their jobs:

   Pet   *Job*

   (canary)   (to make the computer work)

   (eel)   (to teach singing)

   (octopus)   (to help with crossing the road)

   (zebra)   (to make ink)

6. Do you think the class will be pleased if their teacher comes back tomorrow?

   Explain why, using ideas from the poem.

   _____

   _____

Unit 9 Writing a new poem based on a model

In this unit children will:

- read a humorous poem with a lot of word play
- consider the structure of the poem, identifying the introduction and the summary lines, as well as exploring the poet's use of rhyme and rhythm
- recognise the punctuation conventions of poems
- plan, draft, edit and improve a poem about a parent/carer based on the model text.

Stage 1: Responding to the text

Activities:

- In groups, ask children to list all the things they think their teacher has to do at school every day. Ask them to think about:
  - different ways in which he/she teaches (groups, whiteboard, individuals, talking, reading aloud, etc.)
  - daily jobs he/she does like doing the register
  - classroom management organisation/behaviour management roles he/she does
  - other things he/she does around school (playground duties, assemblies, etc.)
  - things he/she does after the children have gone home (meetings, marking books, etc.).
    - Let children share their lists with the class.
- Introduce David Orme as a poet and author who writes manga-style comic books, books and poems for children. He often writes humorous poems.
- Before you read, show the children images of an adder, reed bunting, canary, electric eel, secretary bird (and any other animal they might not recognise).
  - Read *The Teacher's Day in Bed* together and talk about it:
    - Do children think this is a funny poem or a serious one? Why? Can they find something that might be funny?
    - Which line did they enjoy most? Why?
  - Introduce the word 'pun' and explain that it is a word with more than one meaning. Can they find any words like that in the poem (e.g. "*adder*" = snake and someone who adds; "*reed*" = a kind of grass and (different spelling) something people enjoy doing with books).
- Ask children to answer the reading comprehension questions to ensure close reading of the poem and good understanding.
- Together, share answers to the questions and discuss the strategies children used to answer them.

Resources needed:

Shared copy of the text (PDF/IWB/visualiser)

Images of animals mentioned in the text

Each group needs:

- large paper and marker pens

Each child needs:

- a copy of the text
- a copy of the comprehension questions.

Stage 2: Analysing the poem's content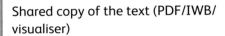

Activities:

- Ask children to read the poem aloud to a response partner in order to revisit the text, develop fluency, ensure accurate pronunciation of all words and to practise reading with fluency, rhythm and a reasonable speaking pace.
- Tell children to underline any new words or phrases. Take feedback and explain what these mean in context.

Discussing the meaning of the poem

- *Think, pair, share:* Do you think the poet knows what goes on in a classroom today?
  - Ask children to underline:
    - jobs that were on their lists from Stage 1 (above)
    - jobs that their teacher does in one colour and jobs that he/she doesn't do in another.
  - Think about *why* the poet chose to include the things your teacher doesn't do (e.g. *because they do in some schools; because he's remembering when he was at school; because he thought the ideas were funny and wanted to include them*).
- In their pairs, ask children to look carefully at the creatures chosen for each job. Can they think of three creatures who would do a job just as well as the one listed? (E.g. *A lion could keep order at the front; an alligator or a piranha could sharpen the pencils by gnawing at them with their sharp teeth; a dolphin could give swimming lessons*, etc.)
- *Think, pair, share:* Ask children to look back at the lists they made at Stage 1 (above). Look at other jobs teachers do that aren't in the poem. Can they think of other creatures who could do them? (E.g. *A chimpanzee to teach PE; a penguin could do playground duty in winter*, etc.)

Talking about the structure of the poem

- The poem is divided into four segments. Ask children to:
  - read each one separately and consider its function (e.g. *opening two lines are an introduction; "There's" is the beginning of the sentence with the list in it; the long section is the list of animals and their jobs; the final two lines are a summary, pointing out the number of different jobs a teacher does*).

Resources needed:

Shared copy of the text (PDF/IWB/visualiser)

Each pair needs:

- an additional copy of the poem
- scissors

Each child needs:

- their own copy of the text
- additional paper for making notes
- different coloured pens/pencils.

Stage 3: Analysing the text structure and language

Activities:

Evaluating verse structure

- Let groups annotate the enlarged poem.
- Ask them where in a line of a poem they would look for rhyming words. (*The end.*)
  - Can they find pairs of rhyming words? (*"In bed/instead"; "knew/do".*)
  - Where in the poem are these rhyming words? (*The first and last verses.*)
- What do children know about rhythm and beat? (*Rhythm reflects all the syllables of every word and beat is the steady pulse that you can clap.*)

Resources needed:

Shared copy of the text (PDF/IWB/visualiser)

Each group needs:

- an enlarged A3 copy of the poem
- highlighter pens

Each child needs:

- a copy of the text
- different coloured highlighters/pens/pencils.

- In pairs, ask children to try clapping the rhythm and beat of the first two lines.
  - One should practise clapping the steady beat:
    - four beats: *Our TEACHer's HAVing a DAY in BED*
      She's SENT her PETS to SCHOOL inSTEAD
  - The other should clap the rhythm:
    - (*di DUM di DUM di di DUM di DUM*
      di DUM di DUM di DUM di DUM).
  - Once children have practised in pairs, try clapping together.
  - Let children swap roles to clap the beat and the rhythm of the last two lines.
- Ask children if there is a regular rhythm or beat to the long verse. (*There isn't.*)
  - Can they find a pattern which isn't rhyme, rhythm or beat? (*The pattern is in the language. Most lines begin "An [animal] to …"*)
- Ask children why they think the poet chose to have a rhyming and rhythmical first and last verse, and a main verse which is neither but which has patterned language.

Looking at punctuation

- In pairs, ask children to highlight all the punctuation marks.
  - Which punctuation marks are used most often in this poem? (*Commas.*) Why? (*Because most of the poem is a list.*)
  - Let children read the poem aloud to each other, thinking about how we use both line length and punctuation to guide intonation.
  - *Think, pair, share:* Did you find line length or punctuation most useful in helping you to read the poem?
- Ask children why they think there are more capital letters than full stops in this poem. (*Remind them of the convention of starting each new line with a capital letter.*)
- Ask children to find question marks and exclamation marks in the poem. Ask how the punctuation changes the way they read the lines aloud.
- Together, discuss why understanding the punctuation can make it easier to understand the meaning of a poem.

Looking at sentences

- Check that children understand that the function of *"There's …"* is to introduce all the items in the list.
- The poet could have chosen to repeat *"There's"* at the beginning of every line. Why do you think he didn't? (E.g. *It would be too repetitious; it would get in the way of the humour.*)
- *Think, pair, share:* Ask children to count the number of sentences in the poem (*there are five: the first verse; the last verse; the long verse beginning "There's" and the two sentences in brackets*).

Looking at "A" and "An"

- Ask children to use:
  - one colour to circle all the noun phrases beginning with "A" (*most lines*)
  - another colour to circle all the noun phrases beginning with "An" ("*An adder*", "*An octopus*", "*An elephant*", "*An electric eel*").
- Can they explain why some lines start with "A" and some start with "An" ("*An*" *precedes a noun starting with a vowel sound*).
- Can they suggest other animal names that would need *An* in front of them? (E.g. *antelope, armadillo, eagle, elk, iguana, impala, orca, orangutan.*)

Stage 4: Planning to write: Writing a new poem based on a model

Activities:

- In groups ask children to:
  - list the jobs that their main carer (parent, grandparent, foster carer, etc.) does for the household. They should think about:
    - activities in the house (e.g. *cleaning, mending, laundry, washing up, cooking, tidying*)
    - activities with/for people (e.g. *cooking, comforting, sharing, helping, organising, bossing*)
    - activities outside of the house (e.g. *shopping, driving*)
    - personal activities (e.g. *meeting with friends, watching TV, social media, shopping, sports*).
  - Individual children should write the names of animals which might be good at each job on sticky notes and stick them beside the job. Encourage children to place their sticky note beside the job they thought of it for, even if someone else has already suggested an animal for that job.
- Give children time to review the outcomes for their own group and to look at ideas from other groups.
- Distribute the writing framework. Model using it to record some ideas about the jobs you do when you're not in school and which creatures could so some of the tasks.
- Tell children that they should:
  - decide who their poem will be about
  - edit or rewrite the opening verse to make it work for their identified carer
  - carefully choose at least eight jobs, matched to chosen animals – remind children they can use the ideas their group came up with (allow some children to borrow lines from the model poem).
  - edit or rewrite the closing verse to make it work for their identified carer.
- Give children time to share their ideas with a response partner and to receive feedback.
- Ask children what a successful version of this poem would include. Amend the success criteria (online at My Rising Stars) if necessary.
- Clarify the success criteria.

Resources needed:

Shared copy of the text (PDF/IWB/visualiser)

The success criteria

Each group needs:
- large paper
- sticky notes

Each child needs:
- the copy of the text they have previously highlighted and annotated
- the writing framework from page 102 (some children may benefit from this being enlarged to A3) or success criteria if a different writing framework is used.

Stage 5: Writing

Activities:

- Remind children that they are going to write a new poem based on 'The Teacher's Day in Bed'.
- Model using the plan you created at Stage 4 (above). Number the ideas to show the order you plan to use them, then begin to write. Ensure you include an animal that needs the article 'an'.
- Before they start, give children a few minutes to review and number their ideas and to 'talk like a poet' and tell their partner ideas for the lines as they plan to write them. If it helps, ask them to use a polite 'writer's voice'.
- Let response partners give some brief feedback before children swap roles.
- Read aloud the success criteria (online at My Rising Stars).
- Let the children write. Break up the process. Quickly model a line or idea, or remind the children to use an animal beginning with a vowel sound, so they can try ideas out in their writing.
- Five minutes before the end of the session, ask all children to stop writing and read their text aloud to themselves. If they find errors, or missing words or words they can improve, they should use this opportunity to make changes.

Resources needed:

The success criteria

Each child needs:
- the copy of the poem they have previously annotated
- the completed and annotated writing framework, including the success criteria.

Stage 6: Improving, editing, reviewing and sharing the writing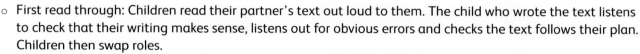

Activities:

- Revisit together the success criteria (online at My Rising Stars).
- Model the process below using your work as an example. The children can give you feedback on each step of the process. After you model a step, the children should have a go with their partner at editing their own work.
- Ask children to reread their texts three times with their response partner:
  - First read through: Children read their partner's text out loud to them. The child who wrote the text listens to check that their writing makes sense, listens out for obvious errors and checks the text follows their plan. Children then swap roles.
  - Second read through: Children read their partner's text and highlight the success criteria they have met. They suggest three places where their partner could improve their work (to achieve or further improve on the success criteria).
  - Third read through: Children proofread their partner's text together with them. They check for errors in punctuation and spelling and correct these as necessary. You should give input at this stage if needed.

Resources needed:

Each child needs:

- the success criteria
- their writing/completed writing framework
- different coloured highlighters/pens/pencils.

Lessons from writing

- Prior to the session, identify errors that were commonly made. Write sample sentences that need to be corrected and ask the children to help you to fix them. These could include:
  - not matching an animal with a job, e.g. *A snake to play football.*
    - Ask children to think of characteristics of a good football player: runs fast, good at kicking.
    - Which creatures might be better suited to playing football? (E.g. *a horse, ostrich or camel.*)
  - helping children to 'see' opportunities for possible puns, e.g.
    - *A lion to stop people lion [lying] around lazily*
    - *A bear to make life bearable*
    - *An elephant to spot things that are irrelephant [irrelevant]*
    - *A panda to sort out any pandamonium [pandemonium]*
    - *A porpoise to decide whether someone was bad on porpoise [purpose]*
    - *A seal to make seally [silly] remarks*
    - *A lobster to work out who is shellfish [selfish]*
    - *A cow-cultor [calculator] for counting cows.*

    What other ideas can the children suggest?

Improving the writing

- **After the poems have been marked:** give the children time to read through your comments, to look at the success criteria and to implement any changes suggested. This should not involve the children rewriting the entire poem – just those parts that you would like them to revisit to practise/improve their writing. If they have used IT, you may want them to edit using a different colour text.

Share

Sometimes, children write to practise writing. Other times, there is a planned reason or an audience. If you want children to share their writing:

- let them make a presentation copy, perhaps with some border illustrations, as a gift for their carer
- this poem can be the focus of a group performance where each child selects their best line or lines, as poems are often ideal for performance
- make a display using children's illustrations of the different animals doing their jobs and a few lines from each child's poem.

Name: **Class:**   **Date:**

My _____**'s having a day in bed.**

She/He's asked her/his pets to work instead.

There's …

Animal name	Job
E.g. An anteater	to suck up the dirt from the floor

I bet that no one ever knew

Just how many jobs a _____ can do.

Name: Date:

	Contents	Text structure and organisation	Sentence structure	Vocabulary and descriptions	Punctuation	Spelling and handwriting
Working **at greater depth within** the expected standard	The poem includes some 'asides' by the narrator as in the model poem.	The opening and closing rhyming couplets are adapted or rewritten.		There may be some attempt to play with language.	Punctuation of 'asides' may include an attempt to use brackets as shown in the model poem.	Spelling changes needed to add vowel suffixes are often accurate. In handwriting, most letters are appropriately joined or word-processing speed is developing and does not impede thought processes.
Working **at** the expected standard	A funny poem about animals doing jobs they seem adapted for but which are normally done by a carer is written.	The opening and closing rhyming couplets have been amended from the writing framework. The poem has four sections, echoing the model poem.	At least two animal names are correctly preceded by An. Most lines follow the pattern in the model of An [animal] to ….	Accurate and descriptive verbs and nouns are used.	Correct punctuation follows the model text with commas at the end of lines, capitals at the beginning and end of sentence punctuation (.?!) where needed.	Taught spellings from the Year 3/4 word list are correct. Some letters are joined using diagonal or horizontal strokes. Letters and spaces are in proportion to each other.
Working **towards** the expected standard		The poem is at least eight lines long.		Some attempt to use accurate language is made.	Some punctuation is included, based on the model poem.	Spelling errors are phonetically decodable. Spaces between letters and words allow for good legibility.

Answers

Unit 1

1. ✓ a puppy
2. It had a sticking plaster on its paw. It smelled of strawberry shampoo and cheese and pickle sandwiches.
3. She knew that someone loved it.
4. The girl smelled of strawberry shampoo and so did the teddy. The girl was crying.
5. To say thank you.
6. Scout saw the teddy in a puddle.   1
   The school bell rang.   4
   Scout put the teddy on a bench.   2
   Scout took the teddy to the school.   3

Unit 2

1. He was going to see The Stupendous Alacazamo's spectacular live magic show.
2. ✓ He'd saved for months to buy them.
3. found his autograph book; set his trusty old video to record the football.
4. The show was at the Glitterball Theatre.
5. ✓ an excited silence
6. Excited/happy because this was something he'd always dreamed of doing and now it was happening.

Unit 3

1. a climbing frame shaped like a model ship
2. (a) Charlie   (b) Max
3. screamed
4. He was surprised.
5. Because swirling light had appeared behind him and he hadn't seen it.
6. ✓ Colours flashed across it.
   ✓ It spun in a disc shape.
   ✓ It was three metres across.

Unit 4

1. They were getting used to the storm and the darkness.
2. ✓ pale and grey
3. The sound of hooves galloping.
4. ✓ He didn't smile.
   ✓ He was tall.
   ✓ He was a stranger.
5. "Please take Annie to get the doctor. The baby's coming." or any similar answer.
6. Annie was going into Waterslain with the horseman.

Unit 5

1. ✓ They inject a venom into their prey.
   ✓ They are lizards.
   ✓ They live in Indonesia.
2. ✓ relax
3. bright pink
4. Flying dragons use flaps of skin over their ribs to glide from tree to tree.
5. (a) They can puff out their ruff to make a ring of black, spiked scales around their neck.
   (b) No, because they only eat fruit, vegetables and insects or because they are only 60cm long. You could accept 'yes' answers but only if they are justified by evidence from the text.

6. Komodo dragon   1
   Dragonsnake   2
   Dragon millipede   5
   Flying dragon   4
   Bearded dragon   3

Unit 6

1.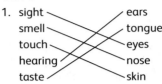
   sight — eyes
   smell — nose
   touch — skin
   hearing — ears
   taste — tongue
2. nerves
3. ✓ cells that can sense what you touch
4. You touch more things with your hands.
5. Messages reach the brain.   4
   Touch receptors sends message along the nerve.   2
   Messages go up the spinal cord.   3
   Something touches the skin.   1
6. ✓ To help the reader understand the text.

Unit 7

1. masses of wildlife or thousands of different types of insects, spiders, woodlice and slugs.
2. ✓ There are thousands of them in every garden.
   ✓ They provide food for bigger creatures
3. Hedgehogs are very good at hiding.
4. Bushes and log piles provide places where hedgehogs can sleep during the day and hibernate in winter.
5. The grey squirrels are more aggressive and have driven the red squirrels away.
6. **Don't like them:** driven red squirrels away; strip bark from trees; take food from bird feeders
   Do like them: funny, entertaining, great acrobats

Unit 8

1. Stick — wing
   Garden fleece — front edge of wing
   Milk container — tail flight
2. The wings must be big enough to lift the plane into the air.
3. Stick a small weight on the machine's nose.
4. So you know when to mark your sundial.
5. To push the stick into to keep it upright if the site has a hard surface.
6. A stick, (a plant pot), chalk or pebbles or short sticks, a clock or watch.

Unit 9

1. Adding is part of maths and an adder can add very well.
2. No because there's a tiger keeping order at the front of the classroom or any similar answers.
3. It could help with reeding/reading
4. Swimming will be taught by a piranha fish – and that's scary.
5. Canary — to teach singing
   Eel — to make ink
   Octopus — to make the computer work
   Zebra — to help with crossing the road
6. Accept a range of answers, e.g. Yes, because she's less scary than her pets – especially the tiger and the crocodile/No, because it must be fun having a dragon to cook your sausages.